noodles

and pasta

noodles
and pasta

Joy Davies

photography by Simon Wheeler

TIME®
LIFE
BOOKS

Alexandria, Virginia

TIME® LIFE BOOKS

Time-Life Books is a division of Time Life Inc.

TIME LIFE INC.
President and CEO: George Artandi

TIME-LIFE CUSTOM PUBLISHING
Vice President and Publisher   Terry Newell
Vice President of Sales
and Marketing   Neil Levin
Project Manager   Jennie Halfant
Director of Acquisitions   Jennifer Pearce
Director of Special Markets   Liz Ziehl

Design   **Town Group Creative**
Editor   **Elsa Petersen-Schepelern**
Editorial Assistant   **Maddalena Bastianelli**
Publishing Director   **Anne Ryland**
Production   **Meryl Silbert**
Food Stylist   **Joy Davies**
Assistant   **Annabel Ford**
Stylists   **Joy Davies and Simon Wheeler**
Author Photograph   **Simon Wheeler**

ISBN 0-7370-0031-7

CIP data available upon publication:
Librarian, Time-Life Books
2000 Duke Street
Alexandria, VA 22314

First published in the United Kingdom in 1999 by
Ryland Peters & Small, Cavendish House, 51–55
Mortimer Street, London W1N 7TD. Text copyright ©
Joy Davies 1999. Design, photographs and
illustrations copyright © Ryland Peters & Small 1999.

Notes
All spoon measurements are level unless otherwise
noted. Specialist Asian ingredients are available in
larger supermarkets, Thai, Chinese, Japanese, and
Vietnamese shops, as well as Asian stores.

contents

Noodles and pasta are ancient foods and there is great debate regarding their origin. Fossilized remains of *orzo*, a rice-shaped pasta still used in Greece, have been found on Cyprus and dated to 2000 BC. In Italy, the Etruscans may have eaten pasta even earlier than this but, according to Reay Tannahill's *Food in History*, the evidence is not wholly convincing. We do know that Imperial Roman households employed Greek tutors, gardeners, and chefs, so they may have brought pasta with them. Contrary to popular myth, Marco Polo did not discover pasta in China in the thirteenth century: his text correctly translated reads that the Chinese had pasta "which is like ours." Indians, Arabs, and Persians were all recorded as eating fine thread-like pasta about 1200 AD.

The Chinese were the first in Asia to make noodles. They did so using rice and wheat flour, but only after the introduction of grain mills from the West around 50 BC. Noodle shops soon proliferated in the towns and cities, offering various kinds of noodle dishes and specializing in meat or vegetable sauces. Originally noodles were for the common people, but by the end of the Han period toward the end of the second century AD, noodles had reached the Emperor's table. Noodles spread throughout the East, made from familiar starches such as rice and wheat flour, and also from buckwheat, potatoes, peas, soy beans, and sweet potatoes.

introduction

noodles

Each area of Asia has its favorite noodle varieties. These can be divided into two main categories, fresh and dried, and into a number of other categories according to the starch used in their manufacture.

Noodle making is an esteemed art and requires a master's skill. To see a noodle maker at work, pulling and twisting a rope of dough in the air and watching it dancing into the finest threads, is pure and utter magic. I am a firm believer in letting experts do certain jobs and noodle making is certainly one of them.

What distinguishes Asian noodles from pasta is the wide variety of flours used; wheat, buckwheat, and rice, as well as starches extracted from mung beans, soy beans, corn, potatoes, and sweet potatoes are all employed. Some Chinese noodles are also flavored with shrimp or squid and the Japanese have a predilection for adding green tea and the fragrant pink perilla leaf (*shiso*) to theirs.

While fresh and dried noodles are interchangeable in recipes, fresh do have a "just made," rustic feel about them and are my preferred choice for simple dishes where texture is all-important.

When choosing which noodles to use, take note of the food of the region. Northern China is wheat country, Southern China and much of Southeast Asia favor rice. I tend to use wheat noodles for heavier sauces—particularly those with meat—and rice noodles for lighter dishes, especially salads.

When cooking noodles, never add salt to the water as this masks their flavor. Use soy, tamari, and Thai fish sauce to provide the essential, last-minute seasoning.

Fresh noodles are best bought from specialist producers—they are widely available in Asian markets. Many varieties of dried noodles, on the other hand, are available everywhere, even in corner stores.

1 **Fresh rice flour noodles** (China).
2 **Fresh udon noodles** made from wheat flour (Japan).
3 **Ricepaper sheets** (Thailand and Vietnam).
4 **Dried beanthread noodles** made from mung bean starch (China).
5 **Dried wheat flour vermicelli** (China).
6 **Dried somen noodles,** (left) made from wheat flour (Japan) and **dried chasoba noodles,** (right) made from buckwheat flour flavored with green tea (Japan).
7 **Dried naengmyun noodles** made with sweet potato starch (Korea).
8 **Dried udon noodles** made from wheat flour (Japan).
9 **Fresh ramen noodles** (foreground) made from wheat flour (Japan) and **fresh egg noodles** (background) made from wheat flour (China).

For preparation and cooking information, please turn to pages 140–141.

1

2

3

4

5

6

7

8

9

pasta

The best-quality manufactured pasta is made from 100 percent durum (hard) wheat, ground to make a gluten-rich flour. Mixed to a dough with water or eggs, pasta can be extruded or rolled, then cut into a vast number of shapes which differ from region to region.

A common misconception is that "fresh" pasta is better than dried: it isn't— it's simply different. I prefer the resilience of top-quality dried pasta to any commercially made "fresh" pasta, many of which are not prepared with top-grade durum wheat and cook to a heavy, soggy mess. Italian pasta manufacturers must, by law, use durum wheat and packages will declare this—they are labeled *pasta di semola de grano duro*.

Of course, if you want to stuff pasta and form it into shapes, or add various flavorings, you must make your own. You are then in charge of the quality of ingredients used, the amount of time you knead the dough, and the thickness and shape you prefer to eat. Homemade pasta is not therefore the same as commercially made "fresh" pasta.

There are scores of different shapes and sizes of pasta. I believe there are no strict rules governing which pasta to match with which sauce, just guidelines, local traditions, and personal preference. Italy can be divided into the butter and cream culture of the North, where ribbon pasta is favored, and the olive-oil culture of the South, where they prefer round pasta, such as spaghetti, spaghettini, and linguine. Shapes such as fusilli, conchiglie, and orecchiette capture sauces in their twists and hollows; the ridged surfaces of rigatoni and penne rigate help sauces adhere. Avoid shapes that don't cook properly like shells or bow ties.

There are hundreds of pasta shapes, many of which have been used in the recipes in this book. Shown right are:

1 **Fresh tagliatelli** is homemade (Step-by-step recipe pages 88–89) and is one of the ribbon pastas. Tagliatelli is often used with the creamy sauces of Northern Italy.

2 **Dried tagliatelli** (left) and **dried tagliatelli verde, flavored with spinach** (right). Pasta doughs can be flavored with many ingredients, ranging from spinach to squid ink (*pasta nera)*.

3 **Dried linguine** (left) and **spaghetti** (right) are two examples of *pasta lunga* (long pasta), and common around the world. These are used with oil-based sauces from Southern Italy.

4 **Dried pappardelle** is one of the widest of the ribbon pastas, often used with game and mushroom sauces.

5 **Dried tagliardi** are small sheet pasta squares.

6 **Lasagne** is best homemade, but some artisanal lasagne can be a useful pantry standby.

7 **Fresh pasta flavored with arugula** (see the Step-by-step recipe pages 16–19).

8 **Dried** *artigianale* (handmade) *pugliese*— similar high-quality hand-made pastas include stracchitelli and maccheroni alla chitarra.

9 **Soup pastas; stelline** (left) and **orzo** (right).

For further information, see pages 140–141.

American cooking is a real mix of Old and New Worlds, for ingredients and cooks have been going back and forth for five centuries. My first American pasta experience was huge, happening as it did in the tiny La Luna restaurant in New York's Little Italy. I recall spaghetti and meatballs, swimming in a lake of rich red tomato sauce that mirrored the colors of the checked tablecloth. I was in New York and Naples at the same time: I could equally have been in Chinatown and eating the best handmade noodles. The tomatoes for my sauce had traveled far, from the New World to the Old and back via Naples. Innovation continues— and pasta and noodles play a large part.

america

rice noodles with
spring vegetables

3 tablespoons extra-virgin olive oil

2 shallots, finely chopped

2 garlic cloves, finely chopped

⅔ cup Shaohsing wine (Chinese rice wine)

1 tablespoon tamari or dark soy sauce

finely grated zest of 1 lemon

finely grated zest of ½ orange

½ cup vegetable stock

3 oz. fine green beans, topped and tailed

8 asparagus spears, sliced diagonally

⅔ cup small fresh peas
or frozen baby peas, thawed

1 small zucchini, finely sliced

8 oz. dried flat rice noodles

a handful of fresh cilantro leaves

To serve:

2 scallions, finely sliced

a few dashes of toasted sesame oil

a few drops of tamari or dark soy sauce

SERVES 4

In the spirit of California with its thriving farmers' markets abundant in vegetables pulled straight from the ground, here is a fresh, light dish that captures the first taste of spring. Keep the vegetables green and choose your own favorites.

Heat the oil in a skillet over medium heat, add the shallots, and cook very gently for 2 minutes until soft and translucent. Add the garlic and cook for 1–2 minutes.

Add the Shaohsing wine, tamari or soy sauce, lemon zest, and orange zest, and bring to a boil. Add the stock and simmer until syrupy.

In a steamer basket set over boiling water, steam the beans and asparagus for about 2 minutes until *al dente*. Add the peas and steam for 2 minutes more. Add the zucchini for the last 30 seconds. Transfer to the skillet and toss well.

Meanwhile, cook the noodles in boiling water for 5 minutes or until tender, then drain. Add to the vegetable mixture, stir in the cilantro, and toss over low heat. Serve on 4 heated plates topped with the scallions and sprinkled with the toasted sesame oil and a little tamari.

arugula pasta with fava beans and tomatoes

The popularity of arugula, which incidentally grows like a weed, has taken off very fast indeed. Flavoring pasta with it, I regret to say, is not my invention but an idea I gleaned from Charlie Trotter, one of the leading lights in modern American food. There are plenty of vegetables here, with flavor accents coming from pancetta, gently sautéed onions, and jewellike vine-ripened tomatoes. The style is fresh, light, and very visual.

1 lb. fava beans, podded

6 tablespoons extra-virgin olive oil

1 small onion, finely chopped

1 thick slice rindless pancetta, finely chopped

2 plum tomatoes, seeded and diced

1 bunch arugula leaves

sea salt and freshly ground black pepper

fresh Parmesan cheese, to serve

Arugula pasta:

¾ cup unbleached all-purpose flour, plus extra for dusting

¾ cup cake flour

2 large eggs

4 oz. arugula, blanched for 1 minute in boiling water, drained, cooled in ice water, then squeezed dry and chopped finely

1 tablespoon extra-virgin olive oil

SERVES 4

1   To make the pasta, sift the two flours into a large bowl. Make a well in the center, add the eggs, then add the blanched arugula and olive oil. Stir well. Knead on a lightly floured surface for 8–10 minutes until smooth and elastic. Cover and let stand for 1 hour.

2   Cut the pasta dough into 4, then roll out and cut as described on pages 88–89.

3   To make the sauce, steam the fava beans for 3–5 minutes until tender. Let cool, then slip each bean from its outer gray shell and discard the shells.

4 Heat 2 tablespoons of the olive oil in a skillet over medium heat, add the onion, and sauté until soft. Add the pancetta and cook until golden. Add the fava beans and tomatoes. Toss to heat through.

5 Cook the pasta in boiling salted water for 2–3 minutes, until *al dente*, then drain and toss with half the vegetable mixture.

6 Heat the remaining vegetable mixture, add the bunch of arugula, and cook until just wilted, about 1 minute.

7 Serve on individual plates and top each with the vegetables and arugula. Serve with flakes of fresh Parmesan and plenty of black pepper.

broiled vegetable
lasagne

My mother made the best lasagne. It took two days and I loved the build-up: the ragù simmering gently for hours, her béchamel tasted like it was made from silk not flour, the giant squares of green pasta bobbing in a sink of cold water, before being immaculately laid out to dry on cloths. I have chosen not to include her lasagne because I now find the dish too rich and heavy—not because I wouldn't be prepared to spend the time making it. Instead I have layered broiled vegetables with a rugged tomato sauce and interspersed the layers with fresh herbs and best mozzarella. I find commercially made lasagne sheets too heavy, so I make my own. The result is a million light years from my mother's dish, but she would love it and I dedicate it to her.

To make the tomato sauce, heat the oil in a skillet, add the onion, and sauté over medium heat for 15–20 minutes until very soft. Add the garlic and cook for 2–3 minutes to soften. Add the tomatoes and oregano and simmer for 20 minutes or until soft. Add salt and pepper to taste and a little water, if necessary, to create a spoonable sauce.

To make the lasagne, roll out the dough and cut sheets to fit a rectangular baking dish, 12 x 8 inches. Bring a large saucepan of water to a boil, add 1 tablespoon of the olive oil, then add the pasta, 3 sheets at a time. Cook 3 minutes, remove, and plunge into cold water. Let dry on a clean cloth.

Preheat the broiler. Mix the lemon juice, garlic, pepper, and 3 tablespoons olive oil in a small bowl and brush over the eggplant and zucchini. Broil for about 3–4 minutes per side, brushing again if necessary until golden brown and tender.

Preheat the oven to 350°F. Brush a rectangular ovenproof dish with a little olive oil and add a thin layer of tomato sauce. Cover with pasta. Arrange a double layer of eggplant on top and sprinkle with mozzarella. Add more pasta, a double layer of zucchini and a layer of tomato sauce. Sprinkle with basil. Add a final layer of pasta and tomato sauce and lots of freshly grated Parmesan.

Bake for 30–35 minutes until browned on top. Remove from the oven, let cool for about 5–10 minutes, then serve.

½ quantity pasta dough (pages 86–89)

¼ cup extra-virgin olive oil

a squeeze of lemon juice

1 garlic clove, stabbed

3–4 eggplants very thinly sliced,
about ⅛ inch

6 zucchini, very thinly sliced,
about ⅛ inch

2 mozzarella cheeses, about 8 oz.,
cut into small dice

12 large fresh basil leaves, torn

½ cup freshly grated Parmesan cheese

sea salt and freshly ground
black pepper

olive oil, for brushing

Tomato sauce:

6 tablespoons extra-virgin olive oil

1 small onion, chopped

3 garlic cloves, finely chopped

10 large well-flavored vine-ripened
plum tomatoes, seeded
and coarsely chopped

1 teaspoon dried oregano

sea salt and freshly ground
black pepper

SERVES 8

1 whole garlic head, cloves
separated but unpeeled

2 sprigs of oregano

¼ cup extra-virgin olive oil

3 strips lime zest

6 well-flavored, sun-ripened
plum tomatoes

2 red bell peppers

4 jalapeño chiles

juice of ½ lime

sea salt and freshly ground
black pepper

1 small chorizo, diced,
or 3 oz. piece of chorizo,
thickly sliced and diced

12 oz. penne

To serve:

a small bunch of fresh cilantro

3–4 blue corn tortilla chips

2 limes, halved

SERVES 4

penne
with roasted tomato,
jalapeño, garlic
and pepper sauce

Penne (Italian for "feather quill") is a short, thick, hollow pasta, often with a ridged surface. It is particularly good for holding heavy or generous sauces.

We are all familiar with the spectacular effect broiling has on raw bell peppers, intensifying their flavor, caramelizing natural sugars, and charring the tough skin so it can be easily peeled away. The same applies to chiles and tomatoes. Roasting garlic transforms it into a mellow purée that adds flavor and thickens at the same time.

The inspiration for this sauce comes from a band of influential American chefs—notably Rick Bayless of the Frontera Grill in Chicago and Mark Miller of the Coyote Cafe in Santa Fe.

Preheat the oven to 350°F. Put the garlic into an ovenproof dish, and add the oregano and oil. Roast for 25 minutes until the garlic is a soft purée (add the lime zest for the last 5 minutes). Remove and let cool.

Meanwhile, broil the whole tomatoes and red peppers, turning them until the skin is blackened and blistered on all sides. Cover and let cool. Broil the chiles, taking care not to burn them or they will taste bitter. Let cool slightly, then peel, core, and chop. Strip the skin from the red peppers, then seed. Peel and seed the broiled tomatoes, reserving some of the skin.

Put the tomatoes and their reserved skins, chiles, and red peppers into a blender. Squeeze the garlic paste out of the papery skin and add, along with the oil from the roasting pan. Blend until smooth. Season with lime juice, salt, and pepper.

Heat the chorizo in a small skillet for 2–3 minutes until the fat begins to run.

Cook the pasta in boiling salted water until *al dente*.

Heat the sauce, add the drained pasta, and toss well. Serve topped with the chorizo and a little of the oil from the skillet, fresh cilantro sprigs, coarsely crumbed tortilla chips, and lime halves.

soba noodles
with salmon sashimi and hijiki seaweed

8 oz. dried soba noodles

1 oz. dried hijiki seaweed, soaked in warm water for 5 minutes, then drained

1 carrot, cut into fine matchsticks

6 oz. very fresh salmon fillet, skinned

Dressing:

1 garlic clove

2½ tablespoons tamari or dark soy sauce

1 tablespoons mirin (sweet rice wine)

1 inch fresh ginger

¾ teaspoon wasabi powder, blended with 1 teaspoon warm water

2 teaspoons sesame oil

To serve:

1 teaspoon wasabi powder, blended with 3 tablespoons tamari or dark soy sauce

3 scallions, finely sliced

1 teaspoon toasted sesame seeds

SERVES 4

The term "Fusion Food" describes a style of cooking in which flavors and ingredients borrowed from one country are interpreted by cooks in another. The result is East-meets-West and in America this trend has developed to a very high level. In this chilled noodle dish, Japanese and American styles meet, and the marriage is perfect. Dried hijiki seaweed, available from Asian stores, has a subtle flavor and is a gentle introduction to the produce from the "sea garden."

Cook the noodles in boiling unsalted water for 4–4½ minutes, adding ½ cup of cold water 2–3 times during cooking. Drain and rinse in cold running water. Chill.

To make the dressing, put the garlic in a small bowl and stab several times with a fork. Add the tamari and mirin. Grate the ginger finely, collect the gratings, and squeeze between your fingers over the bowl to extract the juice. Stir in the wasabi mixture and beat in the sesame oil.

Dry the hijiki on paper towels and put into a bowl with the soba noodles and carrot. Add the dressing and toss well.

Run your fingers along the salmon fillet to check for pin bones and remove them with fine tweezers. Cut the salmon lengthwise into 2–3 strips, depending on thickness, and cut crosswise into ¼-inch pieces.

Arrange the noodles in piles on 4 plates and top with the sliced salmon. Sprinkle with the scallions and sesame seeds, and serve with the extra wasabi and tamari.

Sweet pasta does exist, more usually flavored with cocoa. This is a very subtle pasta lightly sweetened with confectioners' sugar and speckled with the seeds from a vanilla bean. Fresh sweet cherries are gently poached in a rich ruby shiraz (or syrah)—with sweet spices, honey, and citrus. Poached plums or other stone fruits such as peaches or apricots would be good: substitute chardonnay for shiraz.

vanilla pasta
with cherries cooked in shiraz

1 cup red wine, such as shiraz or pinot noir

3 tablespoons flower honey

1 cinnamon stick

2 whole cloves

3 strips orange zest

2 lb. fresh cherries, pitted

confectioners' sugar, for dusting

crème fraîche, to serve

Vanilla pasta:

⅓ cup unbleached all-purpose flour

⅓ cup cake flour

1 large egg

1 tablespoon confectioners' sugar

½ vanilla bean, halved lengthwise

SERVES 8

To make the pasta, sift the flours into a bowl, make a well in the center, and add the egg. Sift over the confectioners' sugar and add the seeds scraped from inside the vanilla bean. Mix, knead, and roll, following the method on pages 88–89. Cut into strips, using the tagliatelle cutter of the pasta machine.

Put the wine, honey, cinnamon stick, cloves, and orange zest into a small saucepan and bring to a boil.

Add the cherries and simmer gently over medium-low heat for 20–30 minutes until tender. Remove the cherries and simmer the sauce for 10–12 minutes until reduced to a light syrup. Remove any foam from the surface, then strain and return the cherries to the sauce.

Meanwhile, cook the pasta in boiling salted water for about 2 minutes or until *al dente*. Drain, refresh with cold water, then dry thoroughly.

Serve on individual plates, topped with the cherries, syrup, and a dusting of confectioners' sugar. Serve with a separate bowl of crème fraîche.

Each of these three countries has its own very different noodle culture. China is the heart of all noodle making, Japan makes noodle eating both home-style and high art, while Korea incorporates its own unique noodles in various soups and stir-fries.

The noodles are varied, thick and thin, and made from rice flour, wheat, buckwheat, sweet potato flour and many other starches. If any dish links all three countries, then it's soup noodle with greens.

china, japan, and korea

Fine wheat noodles are cooked briefly in the Japanese way to keep their bite and texture. They are served chilled on ice, simply seasoned with a selection of accompaniments.

chilled somen with crab and cucumber

Bring a saucepan of water to a boil, then add the noodles. When the water returns to a boil, add ½ cup cold water (this will firm the texture of the noodles). Return to a boil and add a further ½ cup cold water.

Cook for 2 minutes until still firm to the bite. Drain and rinse under cold running water to remove the surface starch. Plunge into ice water.

Mix the dressing ingredients together and divide between 2 bowls. Add the white crabmeat to one bowl and the cucumber to the other (reserve the brown crabmeat for another dish).

Put a layer of ice cubes into 4 bowls, then drain the noodles and arrange over the ice. Top with the crab, cucumber, wakame or spinach, and scallions. Spoon over a little dressing and serve.

6 oz. dried somen noodles

6 oz. fresh lump crabmeat

2 small cucumbers, halved lengthwise, seeded, and very finely sliced

1½ tablespoons dried wakame seaweed, soaked in water for 5 minutes, drained and squeezed dry (or 2 oz. baby spinach, blanched for 1 minute, refreshed in cold water, then squeezed dry)

2 scallions, finely chopped

Ginger dressing:

2 tablespoons rice vinegar

2 teaspoons tamari or dark soy sauce

1½ tablespoons mirin (sweet rice wine)

4 inches fresh ginger, minced, then squeezed to extract juice

SERVES 4

chilled soba
with dipping sauce

12 oz. dried soba noodles

Dipping sauce:

½ cup tamari or dark soy sauce

3 tablespoons mirin (sweet rice wine)

1 tablespoon light soy sauce

1 teaspoon sugar

1 oz. dried bonito flakes

To serve:

1 sheet toasted nori seaweed, snipped into strips

4 scallions, very finely chopped

4 inches daikon radish (mooli), very finely minced

SERVES 4

Elegantly colored soba noodles are made from buckwheat flour. To appreciate their fine flavor and texture, serve them simply—either chilled or at room temperature. Here is a popular and very special summer dish in Tokyo. Everything about it is aesthetically pleasing; the first time I tasted soba, they were presented on a slatted bamboo mat set in a lacquerware box filled with ice, accompanied by a dipping sauce and various condiments. It was so beautiful I wanted to cry.

To make the dipping sauce, put all the ingredients except the bonito flakes into a small saucepan and bring to a boil. Add the bonito flakes and immediately remove from the heat. When the flakes have sunk to the bottom of the pan, strain through a cheesecloth-lined strainer or very fine-meshed strainer. Chill.

Put the soba noodles into a large saucepan of boiling unsalted water and return to a boil. Add ½ cup cold water and return to a boil. Skim off the foam from the surface. Repeat the cold water treatment twice. The noodles should be just cooked (*al dente*) after about 6–7 minutes.

Drain immediately and toss into a bowl of cold water under a running tap. Rinse with your hands to remove the surface starch. Drain well and pat dry with paper towels, then cover and chill until ready to use.

Arrange the noodles in 4 bowls, small plates, or on bamboo mats. Top with the nori strips. Accompany each serving with a small bowl of dipping sauce and a second bowl of scallions and daikon radish to season the sauce.

chilled noodles
with szechuan-style peanut sauce

10 oz. fresh egg noodles or 5 oz. dried

1 teaspoon sesame oil

Szechuan-style peanut sauce:

¼ cup smooth peanut butter

¼ cup tamari or dark soy sauce

2 tablespoons Shaohsing wine (Chinese rice wine) or dry sherry

2 tablespoons toasted sesame oil

1½ inches fresh ginger, minced, then squeezed to extract juice

1 tablespoon rice vinegar

chile oil, to taste

To serve:

4 cups bean sprouts, rinsed and dried

4 scallions, finely sliced

½ small cucumber, finely sliced

1 cake firm tofu (5 oz.) or 1 cooked chicken breast, finely sliced

sprigs of cilantro

toasted sesame seeds

SERVES 4

I remember one bleak, tiring day in the depths of rural Szechuan province, waiting and waiting for a bus to arrive. I spotted a noodle trolley, and my spirits were revived with plain, simple noodles dressed and enlivened by a fiery chile sauce. This is luxurious in comparison, but the taste takes me right back to that moment when everything was suddenly all right. The brown ends should be pinched or trimmed from each bean sprout before serving.

Bring a saucepan of water to a boil, then add the noodles. When the water returns to a boil, cook the noodles for 1–2 minutes for fresh, 4–5 minutes for dried. Drain and rinse under cold running water. Drain again, pat dry with paper towels, and toss with the sesame oil.

To make the sauce, put the peanut butter, tamari or soy sauce, and Shaohsing wine or sherry into a small saucepan. Heat gently, stirring. Add the sesame oil, ginger juice, rice vinegar, and chile oil to taste. Let cool.

Toss the noodles with the sauce. Top with the bean sprouts, scallions, cucumber, tofu or chicken, cilantro, and a light sprinkling of sesame seeds, then serve.

wonton soup

Chinese wonton dumplings are first cousins to other filled pasta shapes like Jewish kreplach or Italian tortellini. Wonton skins, made from egg noodle dough, can be bought fresh from Chinese grocers, pre-cut into squares. Packets vary, but contain about 40 large (4-inch) or 70 small (3-inch) skins. Leftover skins can be frozen. They are served here with Chinese greens in chicken stock, but can also be deep-fried and served with a sweet and sour sauce.

24 small wonton skins

3 oz. baby bok choy, leaves separated, or baby spinach leaves

2 scallions, sliced diagonally

4 cups chicken stock

sea salt

chile oil, to taste

Wonton filling::

3 oz. uncooked shrimp, peeled, deveined, and finely chopped

½ cup ground pork

2 scallions, finely chopped

1 tablespoon finely chopped bamboo shoot

1 egg, separated

½ teaspoon sesame oil

1 teaspoon Shaohsing wine (Chinese rice wine) or dry sherry

1 teaspoon light soy sauce

Dipping sauce:

¼ cup dark soy sauce

1 tablespoon toasted sesame oil

SERVES 4

1 To make the filling, mix the shrimp and pork with the chopped scallions and bamboo shoot. Add the egg yolk, sesame oil, Shaohsing wine, and soy sauce. Mix well until evenly blended. Chill for 30 minutes to firm the mixture.

2 To make the dumplings, put a small teaspoon of the mixture in the center of 1 wonton skin. Brush beaten egg white along 2 of the edges. Press the edges together to make a triangle and press well to seal. Dab a little egg white on one of the points and press the two points together to seal. Repeat until all the wontons have been made.

3 Bring a large saucepan of water to a boil, add the bok choy, and blanch for 1 minute. Remove with a strainer and plunge into ice water.

4 Return the water to a boil and add the wontons in batches. Simmer for 4–5 minutes. Bring the stock to a boil in a separate saucepan.

5 Put 6 dumplings into each soup bowl, top with the bok choy and finely sliced scallions, then ladle over the boiling stock. Season with chile oil. Mix the soy sauce and sesame oil together in a small dipping bowl and serve with the soup.

Ramen noodles are used here—a light, tender wheat noodle that will not overpower the delicate and seasonal sansai (mountain vegetables). Seasonal food is revered and celebrated all over Japan. Weekends involve journeys to the countryside to eat a particular dish, such as an exquisite river fish threaded onto a bamboo skewer as if still swimming. Another favorite is sansai, the young shoots of plants such as bracken, ostrich fern, dog's tooth violet, water dropwort, mugwort, and bamboo grass. Sansai, available commercially from Japanese stores, includes a selection of ferns, mushrooms, and bamboo shoots.

ramen in broth

with greens

To make the stock, put the dashi, tamari, and mirin into a saucepan, bring to a boil and simmer for 5–6 minutes. Add the mushrooms and cook for 2–3 minutes.

Bring a large saucepan of unsalted water to a boil, then add the noodles and cook for about 4–5 minutes until tender. Drain and tip into a bowl of cold water set under cold running water. Using your hands, carefully rinse the noodles of excess surface starch. Drain again.

Bring a large skillet of water to a boil. Carefully prick the quails' eggs with the point of a sharp knife, piercing the tough inner membrane. Crack the eggs into the simmering water, cover, and immediately remove from the heat. Let stand for 1 minute until just set, then transfer to a bowl of cold water to arrest cooking. If using hens' eggs, cook for 4 minutes, then transfer to cold water.

Return the stock to a boil, add the noodles and pickled vegetables or spinach and bamboo shoot, and reheat for 1 minute. Divide between 4 heated soup bowls, top with the poached eggs and scallions, then serve.

7 cups dashi (see right)

2 tablespoons tamari (Japanese soy sauce), or dark soy sauce

1½ tablespoons mirin (sweet rice wine)

2 fresh shiitake mushrooms, finely sliced

6 oz. dried ramen noodles

8 quails' eggs or 4 hens' eggs

8 oz. pickled Japanese wild vegetables (sansai) or 7 oz. baby spinach mixed with 1 oz. chopped bamboo shoot

2 scallions, finely sliced diagonally

SERVES 4

dashi

This all-purpose Japanese stock used
in soups and sauces is made from
giant kelp (*konbu*) and dried bonito
shavings. Instant dashi cannot
compare with the subtlety of fresh
and also contains added MSG.

To make your own, wipe a 9-inch
strip of *konbu* with a damp cloth.
Put it into a saucepan with 4 cups
cold water and heat gently. When
bubbles appear around the edge of
the pan, remove from the heat.
The *konbu* should be soft enough
to cut with your thumbnail: if not,
heat for a further minute. Remove
from the heat and let stand for 10
minutes. Remove the *konbu* and
reserve for a second batch. Bring
the water to a boil, add ½ cup cold
water and 1 oz. bonito flakes.
Return to a boil and immediately
remove from the heat. Skim off
any froth or scum. When the
bonito flakes have settled to the
bottom, strain the stock through a
cheesecloth-lined strainer. Reserve
the bonito flakes for a second
batch of dashi, then discard.
Dashi will keep for 3 days if
covered and chilled.

**EACH BATCH MAKES
ABOUT 4 CUPS**

Ho fun noodles are broad ribbons made from rice flour and sold fresh or dried in Chinese stores. When wrapped around barbecue pork, beef, or shrimp, the same dough is known as cheung fun (stuffed noodle), a popular dim sum dish. Fresh sheets of dough are also sold wrapped up like a book to be sliced with a knife or scissors. They make a real peasant dish, with assertive flavors against a background of soft, slippery-textured ho fun. If you can't find preserved mustard cabbage (in cans or packages), stir-fry bok choy and season with rice vinegar.

ho fun noodles
with beef and preserved cabbage

8 oz. fresh ho fun rice noodles

7 oz. bottom round steak

2 teaspoons dark soy sauce

3 teaspoons toasted sesame oil

3 tablespoons peanut oil

4 oz. preserved mustard cabbage

2 garlic cloves, crushed

1 inch fresh ginger, finely chopped

1 dried red chile, cored and chopped

1 red bell pepper, seeded and thickly sliced

1 small onion, cut into thin wedges

2 teaspoons Shaohsing wine (Chinese rice wine) or dry sherry

1 tablespoon light soy sauce

1 teaspoon chile oil

a pinch of ground Szechuan peppercorns

Put the noodles in a bowl, cover with hot water, and soak for 5 minutes. Separate the strands with chopsticks, then drain, refresh with cold water, and set aside.

Cut the beef across the grain into thin ribbons. Put it in a dish, add the soy sauce and 2 teaspoons of the sesame oil, and turn to coat well. Cover and marinate for 20 minutes.

Heat a wok, add 1 tablespoon of the peanut oil, and stir-fry the beef until it loses its red color. Remove with a slotted spoon and set aside.

Rinse the preserved cabbage in cold water, then drain and chop finely. Wipe out the wok and reheat. Add the remaining peanut oil and stir-fry the garlic, ginger, chile, and red bell pepper for 1 minute. Add the onion and preserved cabbage and stir-fry for a further minute. Add the Shaohsing wine, soy sauce, and chile oil. Toss well and sprinkle with the Szechuan pepper and remaining sesame oil.

Pour boiling water over the noodles, then drain and divide between 4 bowls. Top with the beef mixture and serve.

SERVES 4

pan-fried noodles
with mixed seafood
and black beans

Quickly sautéing a cake of noodles creates the wonderful contrast of crisp and toasted outside and tender inside. This is not as difficult as it sounds, if the noodle cake is allowed to dry for an hour or so, then added to very hot, almost smoking oil. The best black beans—dried and salted—are only available from Chinese and Asian stores. Black bean sauce from supermarkets is a poor, gluey alternative.

To make the noodle cake, bring a saucepan of unsalted water to a boil, add the vermicelli noodles and cook until tender, about 2½–4 minutes if fresh, and 4½–5 minutes if dried. Drain, rinse in cold water, then drain again.

Form the drained noodles into a thin cake, put it on a flat plate, and let dry for 1–1½ hours, turning once.

When ready to cook, heat a large skillet, add 4 tablespoons of the oil, heat until almost smoking, add the noodles and cook for 1½–2 minutes on each side until golden. Transfer to a baking tray and put in a low oven to keep them warm while you prepare the other ingredients.

Mix the sauce ingredients together in a bowl and set aside.

Heat the wok, add the remaining oil and stir-fry the shrimp and fish balls until the shrimp turn just pink, about 1–2 minutes. Add the scallops and toss for about 30 seconds. Remove with a slotted spoon.

Add the ginger, garlic, and chile and stir-fry for 1 minute. Add the bean sprouts and toss for 30 seconds.

Add the sauce and let bubble. Return the seafood to the wok, add the scallions and toss until they turn bright green.

Using scissors, cut the noodle cake into 4 or 6 portions, put onto a heated plate, top with the seafood mixture, then serve.

7 oz. Chinese egg vermicelli
noodles, fresh or dried

6 tablespoons peanut oil

12 uncooked shrimp,
peeled and deveined

6 fish balls, thickly sliced
(available from Chinese shops)

4 scallops, cut crosswise
into 2–3 disks

1½ inches fresh ginger, sliced

3 garlic cloves, finely sliced

1 hot chile,
cored and finely chopped

8 oz. fresh bean sprouts,
rinsed and dried

8 scallions, sliced diagonally

Black bean sauce:

1 tablespoon dark soy sauce

2 teaspoons light soy sauce

1 teaspoon sesame oil

½ cup chicken stock

2 tablespoons Shaohsing wine
(Chinese rice wine) or dry sherry

2 tablespoons salted black beans,
rinsed and drained

**SERVES 4 OR 6 AS PART
OF A CHINESE MEAL**

Kashgar is a wild, medieval place on China's northwest frontier. Its famed bazaar is vast, with avenues of pots, pans, dried chameleons, carpets, spices, vegetables, meat, hats, boots, and more. On the fringe there's the livestock market where men in fur hats test-drive horses at great speed. There are tea stalls, dumpling tents, and noodle shops, where you can watch noodles being pulled and twisted into fine ropes and served with a robust lamb sauce. Such a sauce needs a substantial noodle, like these thick wheat flour strands.

kashgar
noodles

11 oz. lamb shoulder

2 tablespoons peanut oil*

2 red onions, sliced

2 green bell peppers, cored and cubed

2 garlic cloves, chopped

1½ teaspoons ground cumin

1 teaspoon ground allspice

1 lb. very ripe, well-flavored tomatoes, seeded and coarsely chopped

1 lb. thick fresh Chinese wheat noodles

sea salt and freshly ground black pepper

SERVES 4

Trim the fat from the lamb and reserve if preferred (see note below). Cut the meat across the grain into ⅛-inch ribbons about 1¼ inches long.

Heat the peanut oil in a wok, add the onions and bell peppers, and stir-fry for about 2 minutes until the onions are transparent but not soft. Add the garlic and cook for 30 seconds. Push the mixture to one side of the wok, add the lamb, and cook until sealed on all sides.

Add the cumin and allspice, cook for 1 minute to release the aromatic oils, then stir in the tomatoes and 2 tablespoons water. Cover and simmer for 5 minutes. Season with salt and freshly ground black pepper.

Meanwhile, bring a large saucepan of salted water to a boil, plunge in the noodles and cook for 2 minutes until *al dente*. Drain thoroughly, then divide the noodles between 4 heated soup plates and top with the lamb sauce.

*Note: A more traditional method is to chop the fat trimmed from the lamb, add it to the wok, and cook over medium heat until it melts. Use the fat as a cooking medium in place of the peanut oil.

chap chae

2 dried Chinese black mushrooms

4 oz. beef flank steak, finely sliced across the grain, then cut in ⅛-inch strips

2 oz. Korean or Chinese cellophane noodles

2 tablespoons sesame oil

1 onion, finely sliced

1 carrot, finely sliced

4 oz. white cabbage, finely sliced

1 small zucchini, finely sliced

1 bunch watercress, stalks trimmed

Garlic and ginger marinade:

2 garlic cloves, finely chopped

1¼ inches fresh ginger, finely chopped

¼ cup light soy sauce

1½ tablespoons sesame oil

1 teaspoon toasted sesame seeds

2 teaspoons sugar

freshly ground black pepper

To serve:

3 scallions, finely sliced diagonally

2 teaspoons toasted sesame seeds

chile sauce, to taste

SERVES 4

Here is a popular Korean vegetable and noodle stir-fry. Korean cellophane noodles are made from sweet potato starch and have more resilience than the Chinese mung bean noodles. As in Japan, they are often served cold, though the dish works just as well hot. My first experience of chap chae was after a long bus journey to Sogri-san mountain. My most enduring food memory of that trip was eating these noodles, and the extraordinary purple net curtains of the café in which they were served.

Put the mushrooms in a bowl, cover with warm water, soak for 30 minutes, then drain. Remove and discard the stalks and finely slice the caps. Put into a bowl together with the sliced beef.

Mix the marinade ingredients together, pour half over the beef and mushrooms, and let stand for 1 hour.

Soak the noodles in boiling water for 20 minutes, then drain. Bring a large saucepan of unsalted water to a boil, add the noodles, and cook 4 minutes for Korean noodles, 1 minute for Chinese. Drain and refresh in a bowl of cold water.

Meanwhile, heat a little of the sesame oil in a wok and stir-fry the meat and mushrooms for 2 minutes. Remove from the wok and set aside.

Add a little more sesame oil to the wok and stir-fry the onion, carrot, and cabbage for 2–3 minutes. Add the zucchini, cook for about 30 seconds, then add the remaining marinade and watercress. Toss well, then return the noodles, beef, and mushrooms to the wok and continue tossing until hot.

Serve topped with the scallions, toasted sesame seeds, and a generous spoonful of chile sauce.

udon sukiyaki

This splendid celebration dish, popular in Osaka, is cooked at the table in a *donabe*—a large earthenware pot placed directly over a portable burner. An electric wok or large skillet makes a suitable substitute, though less beautiful. The ingredients used here are merely a guide; choose your own selection. To reduce cooking time at the table, some foods, especially the vegetables, need a preliminary blanching (Step 1, page 52). Keep the chicken separate from the other ingredients and add to the hot stock at the same time as the shiitake mushrooms. When all the ingredients have been cooked and eaten, add the noodles to the pot for the finale. Ladle the stock into the bowls and season to taste.

1 head Chinese cabbage, separated or 14 oz. spinach

8 fresh shiitake mushrooms

8 uncooked shrimp

2 cups small clams in shells, or 4 small squid, with the caps sliced into rings

14 oz. fresh udon noodles, cooked as described on page 140

1 large carrot, thickly sliced and blanched for 5 minutes in boiling water

4 inches daikon radish (mooli), thickly sliced, halved if large, then blanched for 2 minutes in boiling water

4 chicken thighs, skinned, boned, and cut into bite-sized pieces

Seasonings:

4 inches fresh ginger, very finely minced

6–8 scallions, very finely chopped

Japanese 7-spice (*sichimi togarishi*), or freshly ground black pepper

Stock:

6 cups dashi (page 41)

½ cup mirin (sweet rice wine)

½ cup tamari or dark soy sauce

SERVES 8

1 Blanch the Chinese cabbage for 1½ minutes or the spinach for 1 minute in a large saucepan of boiling water. Drain and refresh in a bowl of ice water.

2 Remove the thick central stems from the blanched leaves and stack 3 layers of leaves on a Japanese sushi mat or clean cloth. Roll tightly, squeezing out excess water. Cut the cylinder into short lengths.

3 Remove the stalks from the shiitake mushrooms and, using a small, sharp knife, make a shallow, V-shaped cut in the caps. Slice again to form a decorative cross. This also allows the mushrooms to cook evenly.

4 Peel the shrimp, leaving the tail fins intact. With a small sharp knife slit along the back of the shrimp and remove the black intestinal vein.

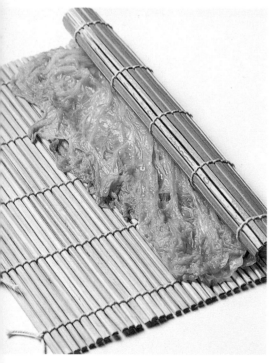

5 Arrange all the ingredients on small plates or a large platter, keeping the chicken separate. Pour the stock ingredients into the *donabe* or casserole and bring to a simmer on top of the stove. Take it to the table and place on the heating unit. Serve each guest a soup bowl so each can take a few ladles of the stock and season to taste.

6 Add a selection of ingredients to the pot, starting with the chicken and mushrooms, and cook for 5 minutes. Cook the squid and clams until the clam shells open fully—about 2 minutes. Cook the shrimp (below) for 2 minutes. Add the vegetables and heat through. Top up with extra dashi during the cooking so the stock doesn't become too concentrated. Finally, add the noodles to heat through in the stock.

Within Southeast Asia, the food link is chile—green, orange, ripe and red, fresh or dried, the scale of the heat varies from hot to explosive. The favored noodles are made from rice flour and their bland flavor and soft texture are the perfect foil for hot, fragrant sauces. This chapter offers the best dishes of the area, which balance sweet, sharp, hot, and sour. And there's one that never fails to surprise—the inimitable Mee Krob.

southeast asia

The Vietnamese flavor palette is one of the most fragrant in all Asia. Who can fail to be tantalized by the balance of hot, sour, sweet, sharp, crisp, and nutty, and rice vermicelli is the perfect delicate base for such a mixture of flavors and textures. This colorful salad excites just by looking at it. Char-grilled sirloin or fillet of beef, cooked rare, can be cut into thin strips and served on top.

rice vermicelli salad

Toast the peanuts in a heavy-bottomed skillet over medium heat until evenly brown. Cool, then rub off the skins, and chop the nuts coarsely.

Plunge the drained noodles into boiling water and cook for 2 minutes. Drain and refresh in cold water. Agitate gently to remove any surface starch. Drain well and toss with 1 teaspoon sesame oil.

To make the dressing, put the lime juice, fish sauce, and sugar in a bowl and stir until dissolved. Bruise the garlic with the blade of a knife, remove the skin, add to the lime juice mixture, and stab several times with a fork to release more flavor. Add the chopped chile and sesame oil.

Stack the lettuce leaves one on top of the other, roll them up, and slice finely. Arrange on individual plates. Put all the remaining vegetables into a salad bowl with the noodles and half the chopped peanuts. Pour over the dressing and toss well. Arrange on top of the lettuce. Serve with lime wedges, chile, and the remaining peanuts.

2 tablespoons shelled
unsalted peanuts

6 oz. rice vermicelli noodles,
soaked in hot water
for 15 minutes

1 teaspoon sesame oil

6 large soft lettuce leaves

2 kirby cucumbers,
halved lengthwise and very
finely sliced

2 carrots, cut into fine
matchstick strips

4 oz. fresh bean sprouts,
rinsed and dried

a small handful of fresh
mint leaves

a large handful of fresh
cilantro leaves

½ small red onion,
very finely sliced

2 scallions, finely sliced

Dressing:

juice of 2 limes

2 tablespoons fish sauce
(Thai or Vietnamese)

2 teaspoons sugar

2 garlic cloves

1–2 fresh hot red chiles,
cored and finely chopped

2 teaspoons toasted sesame oil

To serve:

2 limes, cut in wedges

4 fresh red chiles,
very finely chopped

SERVES 6

vietnamese
spring rolls

This is one of the most interesting forms of noodle—and of using it. Ricepaper sheets are not cooked, just softened in a wide bowl of hot water, then filled and rolled at the table by each guest, ready for dipping.

To make the dipping sauce, dissolve the sugar in the fresh lime juice. Add the fish sauce, sliced chile and garlic, and 2 tablespoons water, pour into small dipping bowls, and let stand to develop the flavors.

Arrange all the remaining ingredients on one or more serving platters, and have a wide bowl of hot water ready for softening the ricepaper sheets.

To assemble the rolls, pass one ricepaper sheet through the hot water until softened, about 30 seconds. Set on a plate. Take a pinch of each of the ingredients—enough to make 1 tablespoon of filling in all—and place in the middle of the sheet. Fold over the bottom edge, then both corners, roll up, dip into the sauce, and eat.

12 ricepaper sheets (3 inches)

½ oz. cellophane noodles (½ small bundle), soaked in boiling water for 20 minutes, drained, then snipped into lengths

1 carrot, finely sliced into matchstick strips

½ kirby cucumber, halved, seeded, and finely sliced into matchsticks

2 scallions, finely sliced into matchsticks

a small handful of fresh mint leaves

a small handful of fresh cilantro leaves

3 oz. fresh bean sprouts, rinsed and dried

6 oz. fresh lump crabmeat, small cooked shrimp, or finely sliced chicken

Dipping sauce:

2 teaspoons superfine sugar

1¼ tablespoons fresh lime juice

1 teaspoon fish sauce (Thai or Vietnamese)

1 small fresh chile, finely sliced

1 small garlic clove, finely sliced

SERVES 4 AS AN APPETIZER

phad thai
fried noodles

Here is the best-known of all Thai noodle dishes. Dried ribbon rice noodles are softened briefly in hot water until tender. They are stir-fried with vegetables, tofu, and pork, then tossed with a sweet, sharp, hot sauce. Crisp bean sprouts, toasted peanuts, scallions, lime, and chile complete the dish. It's a delight.

6 oz. dried flat medium rice noodles

2 tablespoons unsalted shelled peanuts

3 teaspoons superfine sugar

3 tablespoons Thai fish sauce

¼ cup tamarind water (mix 1 tablespoon tamarind pulp with 3 tablespoons water) or vinegar

¼ cup vegetable oil

3 shallots, chopped

4 garlic cloves, chopped

2 oz. pork tenderloin, finely sliced, or uncooked shrimp, peeled, deveined, and chopped

1 cake firm tofu (5 oz.), cubed

1 teaspoon ground chile

2 eggs, beaten

6 oz. fresh bean sprouts, rinsed and dried

4 scallions, sliced diagonally

3 tablespoons dried shrimp, ground in a mortar and pestle or spice grinder

2 limes, cut into wedges

1 red chile, deseeded and chopped

SERVES 4 OR 6
WITH OTHER DISHES

1 Soak the noodles in hot water for 10 minutes until pliable. Drain the noodles, refresh in cold water, and drain thoroughly again.

2 Toast the peanuts in a dry, heavy-bottomed skillet until evenly brown. Let cool, then rub off the skins in a cloth. Coarsely chop the nuts.

(Not shown) Put the sugar, fish sauce, and tamarind water or vinegar in a small saucepan or skillet and heat, stirring, until dissolved.

3 Heat half the oil in a wok and stir-fry the shallots and garlic until lightly colored. Add the pork or shrimp, bean curd, and chile. Stir-fry for a couple of minutes until the pork loses its red color.

4 Add the drained noodles and a little water to stop them sticking. Stir-fry briefly, turning continuously, adding a little more oil if necessary.

5 Push the noodles to one side of the wok and pour in the beaten eggs. Stir to scramble.

6 Add half the bean sprouts and scallions and the fish sauce mixture.

7 Add half the ground shrimps and toss gently. Serve sprinkled with toasted peanuts, the remaining bean sprouts, scallions, dried ground shrimps, fresh lime, and fresh chile.

A popular, visually exciting main course soup, *kao soi* was probably brought over the border into Thailand by the Shan people of Burma. It uses all wheat noodles: in Burma, both wheat and rice noodles are used in the same soup. Eat with chopsticks and a spoon before the crisp noodles have a chance to become soggy. The Burmese would add sliced hard boiled egg to the list of accompaniments.

5 dried red chiles

¼ cup vegetable oil, plus extra for deep-frying

12 oz. fresh egg noodles (*ba mii* or Chinese *lo mein*)

3 tablespoons Thai red curry paste

1 teaspoon ground turmeric

1¾ cups thin coconut milk

1 cup chicken stock

2 tablespoons Thai fish sauce

4 chicken thighs, skinned, boned, and chopped

4 scallions, finely chopped

To serve:

chile oil

4 shallots, preferably pink Asian, finely sliced

3 limes, halved

SERVES 6

Soak the dried chiles in water until softened, about 30 minutes, then pound to a paste with a mortar and pestle. Heat half the oil in small skillet and sauté the paste over low heat until the oil becomes red. Set aside.

Fill a wok one-third full of oil and heat until a piece of noodle will puff up immediately. Add 4 oz. of the noodles and fry until crisp, about 1 minute. Remove and drain on crumpled paper towels. Transfer the oil to another pan to cool.

Heat the remaining oil in the wok and stir-fry the Thai curry paste for 2 minutes. Add the turmeric and stir-fry for about 30 seconds. Add the coconut milk and stock and bring to a boil. Reduce the heat and simmer for 5 minutes. Add the fish sauce and the chicken and simmer for about 5 minutes until cooked through.

Cook the remaining noodles in boiling water, about 1 minute.

Drain and transfer to 4 bowls, spoon over the curry, and top with fried noodles and scallions. Serve with the reserved chile oil, shallots, and lime halves.

thai curry
noodle soup

Noodle soups are served from street carts, in markets, and small cafés all over Asia from dawn to dusk. Cooked rice or wheat noodles are blanched in boiling water and put into a bowl with various additions, such as cooked, shredded chicken or pork, tofu, fish balls, bean sprouts, Asian greens, scallions, fresh cilantro, or mint. Steaming stock is ladled over and the soup is generously seasoned with a spoonful of chile sauce and a wedge of lime. This is Vietnam's version of soup noodle.

vietnamese
soup noodle

8 oz. rice vermicelli noodles

8 cups chicken stock

2 slices fresh ginger

2 chicken breasts, skinned

2 tablespoons fish sauce
(Thai or Vietnamese)

4 oz. fresh bean sprouts,
rinsed and dried

4 oz. young spinach leaves, washed,
dried, and very finely sliced

4 scallions, finely chopped

a large handful of fresh cilantro sprigs,
with stalks, coarsely chopped

12 fresh mint leaves, torn if large

To serve:

fresh lime wedges

2 fresh red chiles, finely sliced

SERVES 6

Soak the noodles in a bowl of hot water for 15–20 minutes. Drain and refresh in a bowl of cold water.

Put the chicken stock and ginger slices in a saucepan and bring to a boil. Add the chicken breasts and fish sauce and poach at a gentle simmer for 15 minutes. Remove, let cool, then pull the chicken into small pieces. Strain the stock.

When ready to serve, plunge the soaked noodles in boiling water for 30 seconds. Drain, divide between 6 deep soup bowls, and place the chicken on top.

Add the bean sprouts, spinach, scallions, cilantro, and mint, then ladle over the boiling stock. Serve with fresh lime wedges and sliced chiles.

The sorcerer's apprentice comes to mind when cooking this spectacular Thai noodle dish— perhaps the most exciting fried noodle recipe. A bundle of fine, transparent rice noodles is dropped into hot oil where it puffs up immediately to fill the wok with a snowy crisp nest. The drama doesn't end there either. The nest is tossed in a sweet and sour syrup, heavy with palm sugar (brown sugar makes a reasonable substitute). I discovered this dish late one night in a dark moody café next to the Mekong River, waiting to cross the border into Laos.

4 oz. dried rice vermicelli noodles

3 tablespoons peanut oil, plus extra, for deep-frying

1½ oz. palm sugar or dark brown sugar

4 garlic cloves, finely chopped

1 small shallot, finely chopped

3 oz. pork tenderloin, finely chopped

6 uncooked shrimp, peeled, deveined, and finely chopped

1 teaspoon ground chile

1 tablespoon rice vinegar

1 tablespoon Thai fish sauce

1 tablespoon lime juice

1 cake firm tofu (5 oz.), cubed and fried until crisp in 2 tablespoons peanut oil

1 bunch fresh cilantro leaves

2 pickled garlic bulbs, finely sliced crosswise into rings (optional)

1 hot chile, cored and finely chopped

2 oz. fresh bean sprouts, rinsed and dried

4 scallions, chopped

SERVES 6 WITH OTHER DISHES

mee krob
crispy fried
thai noodles

1 Fill a sturdy wok or wide, heavy-bottomed saucepan one-third full of peanut oil. Heat the oil to 375°F. Drop in a piece of noodle to test the temperature—it should puff up immediately. When the oil is hot enough, add a bundle of noodles and deep-fry until crisp and barely golden, about 30 seconds. Turn over for a few more seconds.

2 Remove and drain on crumpled paper towels. Transfer the oil to a large saucepan to cool.

3 Put the palm sugar or dark brown sugar in a mortar and pound to a paste with a pestle.

4 Reheat the wok or saucepan, heat 3 tablespoons of the oil, add the garlic and shallots, and sauté until fragrant, about 1 minute. Add the pork and shrimp and stir until the shrimp turn pink.

5 Add the ground chile and toss for 30 seconds.

6 Put the vinegar, fish sauce, and sugar into a small saucepan and dissolve over a low heat. Stir into the wok, let bubble, then add the lime juice. Blend and taste, correcting the seasoning to create a sweet, sour, salty flavor.

7 Roughly break up the fried noodles. Reduce the heat and add to the syrup, turning until the noodles are evenly coated and start to stick together. Add the tofu.

Serve with the pickled garlic, fresh cilantro, chile, bean sprouts, and scallions.

India meets China in Singapore and no more markedly than in this favorite noodle dish. It may be made with rice or egg vermicelli. Buy Chinese barbecued pork from a Chinese store or supermarket.

singapore
fried noodles

2 tablespoons dried shrimp

8 oz. rice or egg vermicelli noodles

3 tablespoons peanut oil

3 garlic cloves, sliced

1¼ inches fresh ginger, finely sliced

1 onion, finely sliced

1 green bell pepper, cored and finely sliced

1 tablespoon hot curry paste

3 oz. *char sui* pork (Chinese barbecued pork) or cooked pork, very finely sliced

2 cups fresh bean sprouts, rinsed and dried

2 tablespoons light soy sauce

6 scallions, finely sliced lengthwise

2 fresh red chiles, cored and very finely chopped

SERVES 4

Put the dried shrimp in a bowl, cover with boiling water, and let soak for 30 minutes.

Soak the noodles in boiling water for 5 minutes. Rinse in cold water and drain. If using egg vermicelli, cook for about 3–4 minutes in boiling water, rinse in cold water, and drain.

Heat a wok, add the oil, and stir-fry the garlic and ginger for 30 seconds. Add the onion, green bell pepper, and drained shrimp and cook for 2 minutes. Add the curry paste and pork and cook for 1 minute. Add the drained noodles and bean sprouts and toss well. Add the soy sauce, scallions, and chiles, and toss until just wilted.

Transfer to a bowl and serve alone or with other dishes.

Muslims in Malaysia and India sauté *sivayyan*—a very fine vermicelli—in ghee, then simmer it in sweetened milk. It can be simply flavored with vanilla or more elaborately with cardamom, saffron, and rosewater. Almonds, cashews, or pistachio nuts and raisins are used as decoration, or for a special effect flakes of silver leaf, called *vaarq*, are added. The pudding is usually served to celebrate the festival of Eid following the fasting month of Ramadan.

indian
sweet vermicelli
pudding

7 tablespoons ghee or unsalted butter

7 oz. Indian or Italian vermicelli, broken into 6-inch pieces

6 cups whole milk

4 tablespoons sugar

a large pinch of saffron threads

¼ teaspoon vanilla extract

¼ teaspoon freshly grated nutmeg

crushed black seeds from 6 green cardamom pods

2 tablespoons pistachio nuts, coarsely chopped

2 tablespoons raisins

SERVES 6

If using butter, melt it in a small saucepan, then strain through cheesecloth. Heat the ghee or butter in a wok or large skillet, then add the vermicelli and sauté until golden brown, about 5 minutes.

Heat the milk in a saucepan, add the sugar, and stir to dissolve. Add the saffron, vanilla, nutmeg, and cardamom.

Add the hot spiced milk to the vermicelli and cook for about 10 minutes until almost tender, stirring occasionally at the start, then more frequently as the milk reduces. Add the nuts and raisins and cook for a few more minutes until the fruit is plump. Serve hot, warm, or chilled.

Italy, or more correctly the regions which make up that most varied of countries, is the home of pasta. This chapter includes a selection of great Italian sauces with some surprises. There are also eclectic dishes from Germany and Spain. Since the Middle Ages, Venice was the gateway of the spice route from the East into Europe and these roots show through in classic Venetian cooking today. The southernmost region of Italy, Calabria, was linked to the East through dishes such as arabiatta, with chile and tomato, which becomes puttanesca when served in Naples (meaning red and hot like the *putte*, or prostitutes, who paraded that most famous of Mediterranean ports).

europe and the middle east

This light minestrone is made with fresh and tender seasonal vegetables and small pasta shapes such as maccheroni or ditalini, which will add body without overpowering the balance of the soup.

¼ cup extra-virgin olive oil

1 onion, chopped

1 celery stalk, chopped

1 carrot, chopped

1 leek, chopped

1 waxy potato, diced

6 ripe tomatoes, halved, seeded, and chopped

1 zucchini, diced

1 bay leaf

a few sprigs fresh parsley

2–3 strips lemon zest

½ cup maccheroni or other small pasta shapes

sea salt and freshly ground black pepper

fresh Parmesan cheese, to serve

SERVES 4

Heat the olive oil in a saucepan over medium heat, add the onion, celery, carrot, leek, and potato and cook gently for 20–25 minutes until softened and just golden.

Add the tomatoes, zucchini, bay leaf, parsley, and lemon zest, cover with water, and heat until simmering.

Add the pasta and cook until tender, about 10 minutes, depending on the size.

Remove the bay leaf, parsley, and lemon zest, taste and adjust the seasoning, and serve with shavings of Parmesan.

minestra di verdure

Pastina refers to all types of tiny pasta used in clear soups. The shapes include the ricelike risone, the star shaped stelline, and the butterfly-shaped farfalline. The world over, pasta or rice in soup is comfort food. Homemade chicken stock is essential. I never used to make my own stock—far too time-consuming and complicated. Now I do, and I'm thrilled to have made the jump. Keep the soup simple or serve it with a few herb leaves, a julienne of vegetables, or a slice or two of fresh truffle.

pastina
in brodo

1 whole chicken, about 3 lb.

1 onion, halved

1 carrot, chopped

a bundle of fresh thyme, parsley, bay leaf, and strip of lemon zest tied together

1 cup soup pasta, such as stelline

sea salt

To serve (optional):

Your choice of:

fresh herb sprigs, a few slices of fresh truffle, or finely sliced strips of carrot, celeriac, or leek, blanched

SERVES 4

Remove any fat from the chicken cavity. Cut the chicken into pieces, then put it into a large saucepan and cover with cold water. Add the onion and carrot. Bring to a boil and remove the foam that rises to the surface. Add 1 cup of cold water to encourage more solids to be thrown off.

Add the bundle of herbs, partly cover the pan with a lid, and simmer very gently for about 3 hours, topping up the liquid as necessary with boiling water. The stock is done when the chicken meat is tasteless.

Strain the stock and discard the solids. Return to a boil and add the pasta. Simmer for 5 minutes or so until the pasta is cooked. Serve as is, or sprinkle with your choice of herbs, truffle, or finely sliced vegetable strips.

This big Tuscan soup is made with white cannellini, brown borlotti or pink cranberry beans. Always use dried beans—the texture and flavor of canned cannot compare.

pasta e fagioli

1 cup dried cannellini beans, soaked overnight in cold water, if you prefer*

1 thick slice rindless pancetta, chopped

4–5 tablespoons extra-virgin olive oil

1 celery stalk, chopped

2 carrots, chopped

2 onions, chopped

2 garlic cloves, chopped

6 ripe, well-flavored tomatoes, seeded and finely chopped

2 sprigs sage or rosemary

1 bay leaf

1 cup short ribbed maccheroni or ditali

sea salt and freshly ground black pepper

To serve:

extra-virgin olive oil

coarse-textured bread, lightly toasted

SERVES 6

Drain and rinse the beans if they have been soaked. Put in a deep saucepan, cover with cold water, and bring to a boil. Cover with a lid and simmer for 1½ hours or until tender. Strain the beans, reserving the cooking water. Remove half the beans and mash or pureé by hand or machine (see note below). Return to the pan with sufficient reserved cooking water to make a thick soup.

Heat the olive oil in a wide saucepan; add the pancetta, celery, carrots, onions, and garlic, and sauté gently for about 25 minutes until soft and golden. Add the tomatoes, sage or rosemary, and bay leaf, and simmer for 20 minutes.

Add the thick bean soup and simmer for an additional 20 minutes to blend the flavors. Add a little more cooking water to the pan and stir in the pasta. Simmer for about 10 minutes, stirring constantly to prevent the pasta from sticking.

Remove from the heat, let stand for 10 minutes, then add salt and pepper to taste. Remove and discard the herb stalks. Serve in deep bowls with a swirl of your best extra-virgin olive oil and some coarse-textured bread, held over a flame to char the edges.

*Note: I have recently been experimenting with bean-cooking methods and whether soaking them first makes any difference. I believe not—without soaking the cooking time is only slightly increased. When cooking beans, keep the pot covered to produce a creamier texture. Mashing the beans by hand will also produce a better texture than processing by machine.

I drew inspiration for this recipe from *eggah*, the traditional Arab omelet, the Italian frittata, and the Spanish tortilla. To intensify its flavor, the pasta can be cooked in chicken stock.

eggah
noodle omelette

3 oz. fine tagliatelli, cooked, drained, and tossed with a little olive oil

2–3 tablespoons extra-virgin olive oil

3 slices bacon, very finely chopped

2 zucchini, finely sliced into matchstick strips

4 large eggs

a handful of chopped fresh parsley

1 tablespoon freshly grated Parmesan cheese

sea salt and freshly ground black pepper

SERVES 6

Heat a well-seasoned or nonstick omelet pan over a medium-high heat, add 2 tablespoons of the oil, heat through, then add the bacon and sauté until golden. Remove and drain on paper towels. Add the zucchini to the pan and cook over a gentle heat until soft but not colored.

Beat the eggs in a bowl, add salt and pepper, then the pasta, bacon, zucchini, and parsley. Stir well.

Heat a little more oil in the pan over medium heat and pour in the mixture, flattening it down slightly. Cook over a gentle heat for 5 minutes or so, lifting the edge with a spatula until the bottom is golden brown. Sprinkle with Parmesan, then put under a hot broiler until golden and puffy. Let cool to room temperature and serve in wedges.

homemade pasta
with truffle

Homemade pasta is made from flour, eggs, and a little extra-virgin olive oil. For the best flavor and texture and a dough that is easier to knead and roll, use a mixture of half unbleached all-purpose flour and half cake flour.

Pasta machines are inexpensive and easy to use, and practice makes perfect.

The simplest dishes demand the best-quality ingredients. Truffles are powerful, complex, enticing, and heady—everyone deserves to eat them at least once in life. This is not an everyday dish—but it is a dish you will never forget.

¾ **cup unbleached all-purpose flour, plus extra for dusting**

¾ **cup cake flour**

2 large eggs

1 tablespoon extra-virgin olive oil

To serve:

extra-virgin olive oil

fresh Parmesan cheese

1 fresh white or black truffle, brushed with a soft brush, then finely sliced

freshly ground black pepper

SERVES 4

1 To make the pasta, sift the two flours into a bowl and make a well in the center.

2 Break in the eggs and add the olive oil. Mix until all the flour has been combined. Add a little water or extra flour, if required. Draw the dough together.

3 Knead on a lightly floured work surface for about 10 minutes until very smooth. Rub the dough with flour, cover with plastic wrap, and let sit for 1 hour.

4 Set up the pasta machine. Cut the dough into 4 pieces and work on one piece at a time. Keep the rest covered. Flatten the dough, lightly dust with flour and put it through the rollers on the widest setting.

5 Fold the pasta sheet into 3, give one turn and run through the rollers again. Continue rolling and folding about 10–12 times until the pasta is very smooth. Rub the sheet with a little flour each time to prevent sticking. Reduce the setting one notch and roll again, this time without folding the dough.

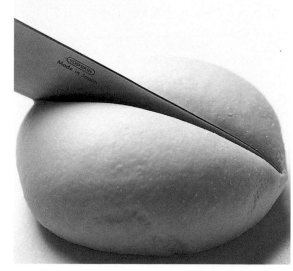

  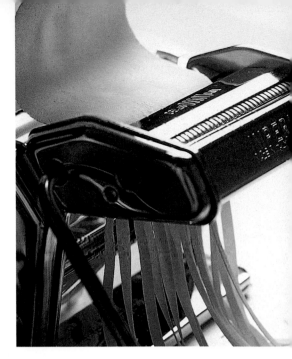

6   Work down through the settings, rolling the pasta through each time until it is as thin as possible.

7   Hang the pasta sheets over 2 poles or the backs of chairs, dusting lightly with flour to prevent sticking. Let dry for 10–12 minutes. (It should not dry so much that it cracks at the edges.)

8   Pass one sheet at a time through the broad cutter to make tagliatelli or the fine cutter for tagliolini. Toss handfuls of the pasta with a little flour and drop loosely in small nests onto a floured cloth. After 24 hours, when completely dry, the pasta will keep in an airtight container for weeks.

9   Bring a large saucepan of salted boiling water to a boil, then drop in the pasta. Return to a boil and simmer for 2–3 minutes until *al dente*. Drain.

10 Add 2 tablespoons extra-virgin olive oil to the pan. Add the pasta and toss well. Serve with shavings of fresh truffle, Parmesan, and freshly ground black pepper, or toss with the sauce of your choice.

8 oz. fresh porcini or chanterelle mushrooms, or 7 oz. cremini mushrooms with ½ oz. dried porcini, rinsed and soaked in warm water for 30 minutes

3 tablespoons extra-virgin olive oil

1 thick slice rindless pancetta, finely chopped

2 garlic cloves, finely chopped

⅔ cup dry white wine

lemon juice, to taste

2 tablespoons chopped fresh parsley

12 oz. pappardelle

freshly ground black pepper

freshly grated Parmesan cheese, to serve

SERVES 4

Wide, flat, dried pappardelle are often used with highly flavored sauces such as game or mushroom. The porcini, *Boletus edulus*, is the king of mushrooms, and matchless when fresh. If unavailable, use cultivated mushrooms with a few dried porcini—they have an incredible, heady aroma.

pappardelle with porcini

Finely slice the fresh mushrooms. If using dried porcini, drain and reserve the soaking liquid, straining to remove grit. Chop the soaked porcini.

Heat the olive oil in a skillet, add the chopped pancetta, and sauté until the fat runs. Add the chopped garlic and cook gently for 1 minute. Add the fresh mushrooms and sauté for 5 minutes. Add the wine, dried porcini, and the soaking liquid, if using, and simmer, covered, for about 15 minutes. Meanwhile, cook the pasta in salted boiling water until *al dente*. Drain, add to the mushroom sauce and toss well. Season with lemon juice and freshly ground black pepper. Serve with freshly grated Parmesan.

6 tablespoons extra-virgin olive oil

3 lb. good-quality Italian canned tomatoes, drained and seeded

8 oz. dried pasta, such as cavatelli or caserechie

sea salt and freshly ground black pepper

freshly grated or shaved Parmesan cheese, to serve

SERVES 4

Of the many variations on the tomato sauce theme, this is the simplest and most powerful. Use very good-quality canned tomatoes: southern Italian are considered the best. When fresh plum tomatoes—genuinely sun-ripened on the vine and grown outside, not in hot houses—are available, substitute the same quantity, halved, cored, and seeded. I prefer this sauce with a handmade pasta shape.

cavatelli with tomato sauce

Heat half the olive oil in a heavy-bottomed saucepan. Add the tomatoes and simmer for 30 minutes, shaking the pan frequently to help release the moisture from the tomatoes and thicken the sauce. Add the remaining oil in stages.

Cook the pasta until *al dente*.

When the oil begins to separate from the tomato pulp, the sauce is ready. Season with salt and freshly ground black pepper, add the cooked, drained pasta and toss well.

Serve with freshly grated or shaved Parmesan cheese.

Variation: Toss 1 cup halved or quartered cherry tomatoes into the finished sauce and cook for 2–3 minutes until slightly softened. Serve topped with fresh basil.

pumpkin ravioli

On Christmas Eve in Mantua, Northern Italy, ravioli are made stuffed with pumpkin mixed with crushed amaretti biscuits, raisins, spice, and *mostarda di cremona* (glacé fruits in a mustard syrup.) So perfect, and so medieval. Pumpkins respond well to such sweet treatment. In this simple filling (even better if made the day before), the flavor of the pumpkin is lifted with nutmeg and mellowed by citrus zest.

1½ lb. fresh pumpkin or butternut squash, halved, with seeds and strings removed

⅓ cup fresh ricotta cheese

½ cup freshly grated Parmesan cheese

grated zest of 1 small lemon

grated zest of ½ orange

a pinch of grated nutmeg

1 egg yolk, plus 1 egg, beaten, for brushing

1 quantity fresh pasta dough (page 86)

sea salt and freshly ground black pepper

all-purpose flour or semolina, for dusting

To serve:

½ cup extra-virgin olive oil

8–12 sage leaves

2 tablespoons freshly grated Parmesan cheese

MAKES ABOUT 60, SERVES 8

1   To make the filling, roast the pumpkin or squash, cut side down, at 350°F for about 45 minutes or until tender. Let cool, spoon out the flesh, and mash with a fork. Mix with the ricotta, Parmesan, lemon and orange zest, nutmeg, egg yolk, salt, and pepper. Chill for 30 minutes.

2   Make the pasta dough (pages 88–89) and roll out to the thinnest setting. Do not hang to dry.

3   Lay 1 pasta strip on a lightly floured surface and trim the ends square. Cut in half to make 2 equal strips. Brush one entire sheet lightly with beaten egg. Put ½ teaspoon of filling at 1-inch intervals about ½ inch from the top edge of the sheet. Make another row underneath, leaving ½ inch between the rows. Take the other pasta strip and, working from one end, press firmly around each mound of filling to seal. Take care not to trap any air.

4   Using a pasta wheel, trim the edges of the whole sheet. Run it lengthwise between the rows and then crosswise to make the ravioli. Dust a single layer with flour or fine semolina to prevent sticking.

5　To cook the ravioli, bring a large saucepan of salted water to a boil. Add 1 tablespoon olive oil and the ravioli and simmer gently for 8–10 minutes.

6　Meanwhile, heat the olive oil in a skillet, add the sage leaves, and simmer in the oil for a couple of minutes until softened.

7　Drain the ravioli. Toss with a little of the sage oil and 2 tablespoons of freshly grated Parmesan cheese, then serve with the remaining oil and sage leaves and freshly ground black pepper.

trenette with
pesto

leaves from 3 oz. fresh basil, washed
and dried in a salad spinner

1 teaspoon sea salt

2 garlic cloves, chopped

½ cup pine nuts

2 tablespoons freshly grated
Parmesan cheese

2 tablespoons freshly grated
Pecorino Romano

¾ cup extra-virgin olive oil

6 waxy potatoes, cut into ¼-inch slices

1 cup fine green beans

1 lb. trenette or linguine

**SERVES 6 AS AN ENTREE,
8 AS AN APPETIZER**

Trenette is the Ligurian version of tagliatelle, and it is always dressed with the region's most famous sauce, pesto. The key ingredients are an abundance of fresh basil, pine nuts, the soft floral-scented local olive oil, and Sardinian Pecorino, a sharp ewe's milk cheese. Many recipes substitute Parmesan or equal quantities of Parmesan and Pecorino Romano, which is stronger than its Sardinian cousin. For the best texture, take the time to pound the ingredients in a mortar—a food processor creates a more "manufactured" result. A few slices of potato and green beans are traditionally added to the cooking water, but I prefer to steam the vegetables to improve their flavor and texture.

To make the pesto, put the basil, sea salt, and garlic into a large mortar and pound with the pestle to form a paste. Add the pine nuts and continue working until the mixture is thoroughly blended. Transfer to a bowl, add the cheeses and beat well. Still beating the mixture, add the olive oil in a thin stream. (If you don't have a very large mortar, work in batches.)

To prepare the vegetables, steam the potatoes for about 10 minutes until tender. Add the beans for the last few minutes.

Cook the pasta until *al dente*. Drain, reserving a ladle of the cooking water.

To serve, stir the cooking water into half the pesto and mix with the pasta, potatoes and beans. Serve each portion with a spoonful of the reserved pesto.

Variations: Instead of some or all of the basil, substitute arugula, watercress, or wild garlic leaves.

Maccheroni alla chitarra is traditionally made by rolling a sheet of pasta dough over a wooden box strung with fine wires—a little like a guitar, or *chitarra*. The wires cut the pasta into square strips, which fall through into the box below. The texture of the pasta is rustic and artisanal and I think it is best appreciated simply adorned with this robust sauce, or alternatively, dressed with olive oil, garlic, and chile.

maccheroni alla chitarra
with tomatoes, anchovies, and olives

8 oz. dried maccheroni alla chitarra

3 salted whole anchovies or 6 fillets

3 tablespoons extra-virgin olive oil

¼ cup kalamata olives, pitted and halved

1 cup ripe cherry tomatoes, halved

a handful of fresh basil, torn (optional)

freshly ground black pepper

fresh Parmesan cheese, to serve

SERVES 4

Cook the pasta in boiling salted water until *al dente*. Drain.

Meanwhile, rinse the anchovies under cold water to remove the salt. Using a sharp knife, slit along the belly and take out the bone. Remove fins and tail. Scrape away any remaining bones, cut into 2 fillets, and coarsely chop.

Put the cooked pasta in a large, warmed serving bowl and toss with the olive oil. Add the anchovies, olives, tomatoes, and basil, if using, and season with plenty of black pepper. Toss well to mix and serve with shavings of fresh Parmesan.

ditali with
cauliflower
and anchovy sauce

1 small head cauliflower, broken into flowerets, green stalks chopped if fresh

3 tablespoons extra-virgin olive oil

1 large onion, finely chopped

6 anchovy fillets, drained and chopped

2 tablespoons pine nuts, toasted in a dry skillet

2 tablespoons currants, soaked in 1 tablespoon hot water for 5 minutes

a large pinch of saffron threads, toasted in a dry skillet, soaked in 1 tablespoon warm water

2½ cups short pasta, such as ditali

½ lemon

salt and freshly ground black pepper

3 tablespoons toasted bread crumbs, to serve

freshly grated Parmesan cheese, to serve

SERVES 6

Here is a big sauce that makes use of the bold and ancient flavors of anchovies, currants, pine nuts, and saffron. Its home is Sicily, where the cauliflowers are bright green tipped with purple. They have a stronger flavor than the white varieties. Small pasta holds the sauce together.

In a vegetable steamer basket, steam the cauliflower (and the stalks, if using) for about 10 minutes until just tender. Reserve the steaming water.

Heat the olive oil in a skillet over medium heat, add the onion, and sauté for 15–20 minutes until golden. Add the anchovy fillets and let soften in the oil over a medium to low heat. Add the pine nuts, drained currants, and saffron and its soaking liquid. Simmer, stirring, until well mixed.

Add the cauliflower and stir gently in the sauce. Let cook over a low heat. Meanwhile, cook the pasta in the reserved cauliflower cooking water, topping up with boiling water if necessary, until *al dente*. Drain the pasta, reserving a ladle of the cooking water. Add to the sauce, then add the pasta and toss well.

Season with lemon juice, salt, and freshly ground black pepper. Serve sprinkled with toasted bread crumbs and freshly grated Parmesan.

Visit Venice's ancient Rialto market in early spring and discover wild greens you've never seen. On a recent trip I found *bruscoli*, which look like nettle shoots. A selection of wild and near-wild greens, briefly sautéed and tossed into pasta, is subtle and exciting. Choose from watercress, arugula, nettle or turnip tops, sorrel, fennel, basil, flat-leaf parsley, dandelion, or baby spinach.

spaghettini with wild greens

4 oz. spaghettini

6 tablespoons extra-virgin olive oil

1 garlic clove, finely chopped

2 cups uncooked greens, washed thoroughly, then dried in a salad spinner

2–3 tablespoons freshly grated Parmesan cheese

sea salt and freshly ground black pepper

SERVES 2

Cook the pasta in boiling salted water until *al dente*.

Meanwhile, heat 5 tablespoons of the olive oil in a skillet over medium heat, add the garlic, and sauté for 2–3 minutes until just beginning to color. Add the greens and toss quickly, about 1 minute, until just wilted.

Drain the pasta and toss with the remaining olive oil and 1 tablespoon of the Parmesan.

Add the greens and toss well. Season with salt and freshly ground black pepper and serve with the remaining freshly grated Parmesan.

This Neapolitan dish evokes memories of long days by the sea. Traditionally made with tomatoes, this variation, known as *in bianco*, focuses on the flavor of small, sweet hard-shell clams. Check that the shells are fully shut, or if open, that they will close tightly when tapped. Clams live in sand and can hold a fair amount in their shells so it is important to strain the sauce through a cheesecloth-lined strainer before serving. Spaghettini are the ideal pasta to accompany the sauce.

pasta vongole

2 lb. small hard-shell clams, in the shell

8 oz. spaghettini

¼ cup extra-virgin olive oil, plus extra to serve

2 shallots, finely chopped

2 garlic cloves, finely chopped

about ⅔ cup dry white Italian wine

a large handful of flat-leaf parsley, leaves very finely chopped

freshly ground black pepper

SERVES 4 AS A STARTER

Wash the clams in cold water, discard any that have broken shells or do not close when tapped.

Bring a large saucepan of salted water to a boil, add the pasta, and cook until *al dente*.

Meanwhile, heat half the oil in a large, heavy-bottomed saucepan with a lid, add the shallots and sauté over a medium heat for about 5 minutes until transparent. Add the garlic and cook for a further 2 minutes. Add the wine, bring to a boil, and reduce until almost all the liquid has evaporated.

Add the clams, stirring to coat with the mixture. Cover and cook until the shells open—about 2–3 minutes. Stir a couple of times so that they cook evenly.

Remove the clams with a slotted spoon and strain the juices through a cheesecloth-lined strainer. Return the juices to the heat and simmer 1–2 minutes to reduce.

When the pasta is cooked, drain and add the remaining olive oil to the pan. When hot, add the parsley, pasta, clams, and their strained juices. Toss well, then season with freshly ground black pepper. Serve with your best extra-virgin olive oil, but do not serve with Parmesan.

Forget spaghetti bolognese: this classic, long-simmered meat sauce from Bologna is in a different league and is served locally with tagliatelli—never with spaghetti. I think it also works well with shapes that catch the sauce, such as fusilli or penne rigate. Using half veal and half beef creates a softer-textured sweet sauce. Simmering in milk adds richness and further tenderizes the meat. This is an adaptation of a closely-guarded family recipe.

fusilli with ragù bolognese

6 tablespoons extra-virgin olive oil

1 thick slice rindless pancetta, finely chopped

1 onion, finely chopped

1 carrot, finely chopped

1 celery stalk, finely chopped

8 oz. ground sirloin

8 oz. ground veal

¾ cup dry white wine

¾ cup low-fat milk

2 cups canned Italian tomatoes and juice, strained

1 tablespoon tomato purée

a bundle of herbs (sprigs of parsley tied with 1 bay leaf and 1 sprig rosemary)

1⅔ lb fusilli, penne rigate, or tagliatelle

4 tablespoons freshly grated Parmesan cheese, plus extra to serve

sea salt and freshly ground black pepper

SERVES 8

Heat 4 tablespoons of the oil in a skillet, add the pancetta, and sauté until the fat starts to run. Add the onion, carrot, and celery and cook over medium heat, stirring, until the onion is soft and golden, about 25–30 minutes.

Add the ground meats and cook only until they lose their color. Add the wine and cook until it evaporates. Add the milk and cook until it evaporates.

Add the tomatoes, tomato purée, and bundle of herbs and bring to the boil. Reduce the heat and simmer very, very slowly, partly covered with a lid, for 4–5 hours (the longer the better), stirring occasionally.

Add a little extra water toward the end of the cooking time to prevent the sauce from sticking, then season with salt and freshly ground black pepper.

Cook the pasta until *al dente*. Drain and toss with the remaining olive oil and 1 tablespoon freshly grated Parmesan cheese. Add 1 ladle of sauce per person and toss well. Serve with freshly grated Parmesan.

hungarian tarhonya

1 small Savoy cabbage, cored and finely sliced

3 tablespoons extra-virgin olive oil

8 slices smoked bacon, chopped

2 tablespoons unsalted butter

1 tablespoon sweet paprika

2 tablespoons chopped fresh flat-leaf parsley

sea salt and freshly ground black pepper

Pasta dough:

3 cups unbleached all-purpose flour

1 teaspoon sea salt

4 eggs

SERVES 6–8 AS AN ENTREE: HALVE THE RECIPE TO SERVE AS AN ACCOMPANIMENT

Here is one of the most ancient recipes for pasta. This firm dough is left to rest and dry slightly before grating it straight into simmering water or onto a floured cloth. The tiny grains of pasta have a wonderful handmade texture and can be served simply tossed with butter to accompany a stew—goulash of course would be the perfect choice. Otherwise, serve it with typical Eastern European flavors, such as cabbage, smoked bacon, and paprika.

To make the dough, sift the flour and salt into a large bowl. Make a well in the center, break in the eggs, and mix to a firm dough. Add a little water if necessary. The dough can also be made in a food processor or mixer. Knead lightly on a floured surface for 5 minutes. Cover with a cloth and let stand for 30 minutes.

Grate the dough, using the largest holes on the grater, directly into a large saucepan of boiling water. When the water returns to a boil, cook for 2 minutes. Remove with a slotted spoon and plunge into cold water. Work in batches. (Alternatively, the dough may be grated onto a floured cloth, turned in the flour to prevent sticking, let dry and when ready to cook, boil for 4–5 minutes.)

Steam the cabbage until tender, about 5–6 minutes.

Heat 2 tablespoons of the olive oil in a saucepan, add the bacon, and sauté for about 5 minutes until the fat begins to run.

Heat the butter and 1 tablespoon olive oil in a separate pan. Add the drained tarhonya and toss to coat. Add the paprika, bacon, and seasoning, and stir well. Toss with the cabbage and serve with the chopped parsley.

spätzle

The first time I tasted spätzle was in Bavaria, and I was completely captivated. Tender little dumplings with a definite resilience were tossed with alpine butter and caramelized onions. The pasta mixture is a batter rather than a dough and is scraped into simmering water with great skill from a special wooden board tapered at one end. In Germany, spätzle machines are available for the less skilful cook: they consist of a small metal cup which slides back and forth across a perforated metal plate. Outside Germany potato ricers with interchangeable disks are widely available—use the disk with small, widely spaced holes. Another simple way is to pipe the batter directly into the water using a very fine nozzle.

½ cup good-quality unsalted butter

2 tablespoons extra-virgin olive oil

4 large onions, finely sliced

3½ oz. Gruyère or Emmenthal cheese, grated

3 lemons, halved, to serve

Spätzle batter:

2½ cups unbleached all-purpose flour

½ teaspoon sea salt

4 eggs

SERVES 6

1 Heat half the butter and oil in a skillet, add the onions and sauté very gently until a rich golden brown. Set aside.

2 To make the batter, sift the flour and salt into a large mixing bowl. Make a well in the center and break in the eggs. Add half the water and gradually mix to a smooth paste.

3 Beat well until smooth. Add enough water until the batter just falls from the spoon. (See note.)

4 To cook the spätzle, bring a large saucepan of salted water to a boil. Pour the batter into the bowl of a spätzle machine or potato ricer (see recipe introduction.) Squeeze the batter into the simmering water. If using a piping bag, cut short lengths free with a wet knife. Work in batches.

5 Cook for 2–3 minutes depending on thickness, then remove with a slotted spoon and plunge into a bowl of cold water.

6 When all the batter has been cooked, melt the remaining butter in a skillet, and add the drained spätzle. Toss until heated through.

7 Toss with the onions and cheese and serve immediately or finish under a hot broiler. Serve with lemon halves, for squeezing.

Note: It is impossible to give a precise quantity of water. Much depends on the type of flour used. The thinner the batter, the finer the dumplings.

Rosemary Barron, scholar, cook, and author of *Flavors of Greece* (Penguin 1994), lived on Crete for some years. She tells me archeological evidence suggests that this form of pasta, *kritharaki*, may have been sold in the markets of ancient Greece as an early convenience food. These days you can find it in good Greek or Middle Eastern stores, where you can also buy the cheese. The more aged the cheese the better the flavor: ask to taste it first. Goat's milk butter is the traditional flavoring, which Rosemary interprets very successfully as browned butter and lemon juice.

kritharaki
with brown butter and cheese

1 cup chicken stock or water

1¾ cups medium-sized kritharaki or orzo

5 tablespoons unsalted butter

juice of 1 large lemon

¾ cup finely shredded aged myzithra or kasseri cheese, or other hard sheep or goat's milk cheese

a small handful of fresh herbs, snipped*

a large handful fresh flat-leaf parsley, coarsely chopped

6 scallions, green part only, finely sliced

coarse sea salt and freshly ground black pepper

SERVES 4–6

Pour the stock or water into a large saucepan and bring to a boil. Add the kritharaki or orzo and simmer for about 10 minutes until barely tender. Drain and refresh under cold running water. Drain again.

Gently heat the butter in a small saucepan for about 10 minutes until deep golden brown. Keep the heat very low or the solids in the butter will burn. Strain through 2 layers of cheesecloth into a bowl and add all but 1 teaspoon of the lemon juice.

Return the kritharaki to the pan, add the butter mixture, cheese, herbs, parsley, scallions, and remaining lemon juice. Add salt and pepper to taste. Stir just to mix, heat until warm, and serve at once.

*Note: The choice of herbs depends very much on what is available. How much you use depends on the strength of the individual herb. Suggestions are fresh oregano, chervil, thyme, borage, and cilantro. The mild-flavored herbs can be snipped into small pieces but stronger herbs such as oregano and thyme should be finely chopped.

fideuà

Inspired Valencian cooks used the technique for making paella, substituted short noodles (*fideos*) or fine maccheroni (*spaghetti cortado*) and created fideuà, a dish little known outside its home. *Pimentón*, powdered smoked peppers, can be hot (*picante*) as here, or sweet (*dulce*). It is sold in larger supermarkets, as well as by specialist Spanish grocers. As with paella, to make the best fideuà you must begin with a big fish stock—the locals call this gravy.

a large pinch of saffron threads

¼ cup extra-virgin olive oil

2 oz. monkfish or firm white fish, cut into bite-sized pieces

2 oz. uncooked shrimp, peeled and deveined (optional)

3–4 baby squid, cleaned, caps cut into rings

3 garlic cloves, chopped

1 teaspoon *pimentón picante*

6 ripe well-flavored tomatoes, seeded and chopped

1½ cups maccheroni

lemon halves, to serve

Fish stock:

1–1½ lb. or more fish heads (gills removed) and/or skeletons, from white-fleshed fish

2–3 small squid, cleaned

shrimp shells

1 crab, cleaned, with legs crushed

6 parsley stalks

2–3 strips lemon zest

SERVES 2–3

1 To make the fish stock, put the fish heads and skeletons, squid, shrimp shells, and crab in a large saucepan. Add parsley stalks and strips of lemon zest and cover with cold water. Bring to a boil, skimming the foam from the surface. Simmer for 45 minutes, then strain and discard the solids. Return the stock to the pan and simmer to concentrate the flavor if necessary.

(Not shown) Toast the saffron in a small skillet over medium heat for a couple of minutes to maximize its flavor. Put into a small dish and add a spoonful of water. Let steep.

2 Heat an 8-inch paella pan or similar-sized skillet with ovenproof handles, then add the olive oil. Add the fish and seafood and stir to seal on all sides. Add the garlic and cook for 1 minute. Stir in the *pimentón*.

3 Add the tomatoes, saffron, and liquid and cook for about 5 minutes until the tomatoes become pulpy.

4 Pour the maccheroni in a line down the center of the skillet and stir for a couple of minutes.

5 Add the hot fish stock and stir well. Bring to a boil and reduce the heat.

6 Simmer, without stirring, for 10 minutes or until most of the liquid has been absorbed

(Not shown) Transfer the skillet to a preheated oven and cook at 400°F for 5–10 minutes until the top colors slightly. Let stand for 5 minutes. Serve straight from the pan with lemon halves.

3 cups freshly squeezed orange juice

7 oz. fine tagliatelli

¼ cup dessert wine, such as Spanish moscatel

1 tablespoon blanched almonds, pan-toasted, then coarsely chopped

2–3 tablespoons confectioners' sugar

¼ cup orange liqueur, such as Triple Sec or Grand Marnier

SERVES 6–8

caramelized tagliatelli with orange juice and orange liqueur

Using fruit juice for the sauce in this recipe was the result of a happy accident one day when I was cooking with friends. It is based on the typical Valencian combination of oranges with almonds, and is enhanced by the flavors of Spanish moscatel wine and orange liqueur.

Put the orange juice in a saucepan with 1¼ cups water and bring to a boil. Add the tagliatelli and cook until *al dente*. Drain, reserving the cooking liquid. Refresh the tagliatelle under cold water.

Reheat the cooking liquid and reduce until syrupy, about 25 minutes. Add the dessert wine and bring to a boil.

Preheat the broiler to very hot. Toss the pasta into the sauce, then divide between individual gratin dishes. Sprinkle with the nuts and dust generously with confectioners' sugar. Broil until caramelized.

Warm the liqueur, light carefully with a match, and pour over the pasta while still burning. Serve with a glass of the dessert wine, well chilled.

Another sweet pasta recipe typifies the flavorings of Northern and Central Europe; cinnamon, honey, and lemon. Choose stone fruit in season; plums, peaches, nectarines, apricots, or cherries. Serve with a fruit coulis and a spoonful of crème fraîche, if desired.

noodles with fresh fruit and cinnamon topping

2 lb. plums, halved, pitted, and thickly sliced

1 cinnamon stick

2 strips lemon zest

¼ cup clear honey

4–6 tablespoons unsalted butter

⅓ cup stale bread crumbs

7 oz. tagliardi

1 teaspoon ground cinnamon

SERVES 8–10

Put the plums, cinnamon stick, lemon zest, half the honey, and 1 tablespoon water in a small saucepan and cook for about 5 minutes until the plums have just softened.

Heat half the butter in a small skillet, add the bread crumbs, and cook for 15–20 minutes until golden brown and crisp. Preheat the oven to 350°F.

Cook the tagliardi in boiling salted water until *al dente*, then drain and toss with a little butter.

Put a layer of pasta in the bottom of a buttered ovenproof dish, top with half the fruit, and another layer of pasta. Dribble over the remaining honey and top with the remaining fruit. Sprinkle with the bread crumbs and cinnamon, then bake for 20–30 minutes. Let cool slightly before serving.

Two countries geographically linked from a European perspective have their own very distinctive personalities. Each country displays cooking styles that genuinely integrate European influences with Eastern style. Asian noodles and European pasta are equally important but their seasoning may well be interchangeable. Whatever the mix, it's always exciting and seafood is the star.

australia
and new zealand

American chefs take inspiration from Japan, Mexico, and South America, but Australian chefs look to their near neighbors in Southeast Asia. The result is East-West ingredients with East-West techniques, all on one plate.

tagliarini
with steamed fish and mixed greens

2 fillets firm white fish, such as sole, skinned, halved then cut into 2–3 pieces (about 7 oz.)

2 teaspoons Thai fish sauce

2 teaspoons sesame oil

5 oz. tagliarini

2 tablespoons extra-virgin olive oil

2 garlic cloves, finely sliced

1 inch fresh ginger, finely sliced

10 oz. baby bok choy, cut crosswise into ½-inch pieces

4 scallions, chopped

7 oz. pea shoots or baby spinach, rinsed and kept whole

toasted sesame seeds, to serve

SERVES 4

Put the fish on a heatproof plate and sprinkle with a little of the fish sauce and sesame oil. Set the plate in a bamboo steamer set over a pan of boiling water. Steam for 2–4 minutes, depending on thickness, until the fish turns opaque.

Meanwhile, cook the tagliarini in boiling salted water for 2 minutes, then drain.

While the pasta is cooking, heat a wok, add the olive oil, and stir-fry the garlic and ginger for 30 seconds.

Add the bok choy and stir-fry for 1 minute. Add the remaining fish sauce and toss for 30 seconds. Add the scallions and pea shoots, let wilt slightly, then add the cooked pasta and juices from the steamed fish.

Divide the pasta and green vegetables between 4 heated plates and top with the steamed fish. Serve with a light sprinkling of toasted sesame seeds.

seafood laksa

This main course soup from the street markets and hawker centers of Singapore and Malaysia has become a real Australian favorite. Sweet, sharp, hot, and slightly creamy, the soup is enriched with local macadamia nuts instead of the usual candlenut. One essential, pungent flavor is *blachan*, or fermented shrimp paste, which is available in blocks from Chinese and Asian stores. If unavailable, use 2 anchovy fillets, mashed.

10 oz. fresh rice noodles

2 teaspoons coriander seeds, pan-toasted

3 garlic cloves, chopped

1 inch fresh ginger, chopped

3 fresh red chiles, cored and chopped

4 unsalted macadamia nuts

½ teaspoon *blachan* (shrimp paste)

3 tablespoons peanut oil

1 onion, chopped

½ teaspoon ground turmeric

4 cups coconut milk

1 stalk lemongrass, bruised and cut in 3

16 uncooked shrimp, peeled and deveined

7 oz. fresh bean sprouts, rinsed and dried

3 scallions, chopped

To serve:

a small handful of fresh cilantro leaves

a few dashes of chile oil

1 lime, cut in wedges

SERVES 4

1 Put the noodles in a bowl, cover with boiling water and soak for 5 minutes. Separate the noodles using chopsticks. Drain and refresh in cold water. Set aside.

2 Pound the coriander seeds in a mortar and pestle. Add the garlic, ginger, chiles, macadamia nuts, and *blachan* and pound to a paste.

3 Heat half the oil in a wok or skillet, add the onion, and sauté for 5 minutes until soft and translucent. Add the spice paste and sauté for 2 minutes. Add the turmeric and sauté for 30 seconds. Add the coconut milk and lemongrass, bring to a boil, reduce the heat, and simmer for 10 minutes. Stir in the fish sauce and lime juice.

4 Heat the remaining oil in a separate wok or skillet and stir-fry the shrimp until they turn pink (about 2 minutes.)

5 Add the bean sprouts and scallions and toss for 30 seconds.

(Not shown) Drain the noodles, then pour boiling water over to reheat. Drain again.

6 Divide the noodles between 4 soup bowls. Top with the shrimp and vegetables and ladle over the hot coconut milk mixture. Sprinkle with fresh cilantro and chile oil. Serve with lime wedges.

seared oysters
with rice noodles and vegetables

New Zealand's full-flavored Bluff oysters inspired this dish. A rarity gathered off the southern tip of the South Island, their sweetness and succulence is legendary. Outside Bluff oyster country, I believe it's sacrilege to cook fine-flavored native oysters, so choose rock oysters elsewhere. The silken quality of rice noodles emphasizes the sensuality of this dish.

1 lb. fresh rice noodles

2–3 oz. fresh cilantro

6 tablespoons extra-virgin olive oil

2 tablespoons peanut oil

2 garlic cloves, crushed

1 inch fresh ginger, finely sliced

2 carrots, finely sliced lengthwise

8 scallions, finely sliced lengthwise

12 large oysters, shucked, liquor reserved

2 tablespoons Shaohsing wine (Chinese rice wine)

2 teaspoons fresh lime juice

2 teaspoons light soy sauce

1 teaspoon toasted sesame oil

a dash of chile sauce, plus extra to serve

SERVES 4

Put the noodles in a bowl, cover with boiling water, let steep for 5 minutes, separate with chopsticks, then drain and refresh in cold water.

Blanch the cilantro in boiling water for 10 seconds, then drain and plunge into a bowl of ice water. Remove, squeeze dry in a cloth, then chop. Put in a blender with the olive oil and blend to a purée. Strain into a small bowl.

Heat the peanut oil in a wok or skillet over high heat, add the garlic and ginger, and stir-fry for 30 seconds. Add the carrots and cook for 1 minute. Add the scallions and cook for a further 30 seconds. Add the oysters and strained liquor, the drained noodles, the Shaohsing wine, lime juice, soy sauce, sesame oil, and chile sauce. Toss for 30 seconds. Serve with a drizzle of the cilantro oil and extra chile sauce.

Mexico meets Polynesia in this wonderful example of Pacific-Rim cooking. In traditional Polynesian manner, small cubes of firm white fish are "cooked" in lime juice. Australia and New Zealand have a huge array of fresh fish, and they would use orange roughy, red snapper, or mahi mahi: halibut would give a similar effect. Always choose a firm white fish which is super-fresh (never ever frozen and thawed—that makes for a wooly texture and tasteless flesh.) This recipe uses a fine rice noodle to balance the sharp and the sweet.

pacific seviche
with rice vermicelli

5 oz. rice vermicelli noodles

12 oz. very fresh white fish, skinned, boned, and cut into ½-inch cubes

the juice of 6 limes

2 ripe tomatoes, seeded and finely diced

1–2 hot red chiles, cored and very finely diced

1 tablespoon finely chopped scallion, rinsed under the tap and drained

2 tablespoons finely chopped fresh cilantro, plus extra sprigs, to serve

5 tablespoons coconut cream

¼ cup extra-virgin olive oil

SERVES 4

Soak the noodles in hot water for 15 minutes, then drain and refresh in cold water. Set aside.

Put the fish into a bowl and cover with lime juice. Chill for 3 hours, then drain.

Gently mix the fish, tomatoes, chiles, scallion, and cilantro in a bowl to make a salsa. Blend the coconut cream with the olive oil and stir into the bowl.

Toss the drained noodles with the mixture, then serve with sprigs of cilantro.

Pasta, garlic, and pine nuts from Italy are combined with the Asian flavors of cilantro, soy sauce, sesame oil, Thai basil, and ginger. It's another example of Australia and New Zealand's contribution to Fusion Food.

spaghettini
with asian pesto and prawns

16 uncooked shrimp, peeled and deveined

1 teaspoon lime juice

1 garlic clove, stabbed with a fork

3 tablespoons extra-virgin olive oil

12 oz. spaghettini

Asian pesto:

1 garlic clove, chopped

½ inch fresh ginger, finely chopped

a pinch of sea salt

¼ cup pine nuts, toasted in a dry skillet

a large bunch of cilantro

a small bunch of basil (Thai or sweet)

a small bunch of flat-leaf parsley

juice of ½ lime

1 tablespoon light soy sauce

2 tablespoons toasted sesame oil

SERVES 6–8

To make the Asian pesto, pound the garlic, ginger, and salt with a mortar and pestle. Reserve a few pine nuts for serving, then add the remainder to the pesto with the cilantro, basil, parsley, lime juice, and soy sauce. Process or pound briefly to a coarse purée, then add the sesame oil in a thin stream while still pounding or blending.

To make the marinade for the shrimp, mix the lime juice, garlic, and 2 tablespoons olive oil in a bowl. Add the shrimp, coat well, and let stand for 2 minutes.

Drain the shrimp. Heat the remaining oil in a wok or skillet. Add the shrimp and sauté over a high heat for 2 minutes, until just pink. Remove from the heat.

Meanwhile, cook the pasta in a large saucepan of boiling salted water until *al dente*. Drain, reserving a small ladle of the cooking water. Add the reserved water to the pesto, then toss the pasta and pesto together in a bowl and top with the shrimp. Serve with the extra toasted pine nuts.

sweet potatoes
and chickpeas
with tomato and garganelli

¼ cup extra-virgin olive oil

1 onion, finely chopped

10 oz. orange sweet potato,
cut in ½-inch dice

2 garlic cloves, finely chopped

1 teaspoon toasted cumin seed, ground

1 cup canned tomatoes, chopped

7 oz. cooked chickpeas (garbanzos)*

juice of 2 limes

1 teaspoon hot pepper sauce

6 oz. garganelli or similar rustic shape

2 tablespoons finely chopped
fresh cilantro

freshly ground black pepper

SERVES 4

I first tasted sweet potatoes at a *hangi* (pit barbecue) in New Zealand, where they were buried in the ground on a bed of banana leaves set over hot stones. I will never forget the taste of the sweet, deep orange flesh. In honor of that day, here is sweet potato in another guise.

Heat the olive oil in a skillet over medium heat, add the onion, and sauté until transparent. Add the sweet potato and cook until tender—about 20 minutes. Add the garlic and cumin and cook for 1–2 minutes, then add the tomatoes and 1 tablespoon water and simmer until pulpy. Stir in the chickpeas, juice of 1 lime, and hot pepper sauce and cook for 5 minutes.

Meanwhile, cook the pasta in a large saucepan of boiling salted water until *al dente*, then drain. Add the cilantro and pasta, toss well, season with extra lime juice and freshly ground black pepper, and serve.

***Note**: A refinement to chickpeas – slip off the skins between your fingers before cooking.

varieties, cooking times, and methods

noodles

Asian noodles are sold fresh or dried. Most fresh noodles need an even shorter cooking time than fresh Italian pasta. Some, particularly rice noodles, are simply rinsed in warm water to remove excess starch, stirred to separate the strands, then dunked in boiling water for about 30 seconds to heat through—no need to cook.

As in all cooking, it is the texture and taste of the ingredient, in this case, the noodle, which determines the cooking time. Noodles should be tender, not soggy. Use the following cooking times merely as a general guide.

When soaking dried noodles in water before cooking, the dry weight will at least double after soaking; for example, 4 oz. dried noodles will become 8 oz. when soaked.

china
This country was the source of all noodles in Asia. Its great range of noodle products reflects the differences in climate and culture across the country. Noodles are served toward the end of a Chinese meal.

Thin Wheat Noodles: (egg, wheat flour)
fresh: rinse in warm water, then boil for
     1½–2 minutes
dried: boil for 4½–5 minutes

Thick Wheat Noodles: (egg, wheat flour)
fresh: rinse in warm water, then boil for
     3–4 minutes
dried: boil for 7–9 minutes

Wheat Noodles: (wheat flour)
fresh: rinse in warm water, then boil for
     3–4 minutes
dried: boil for 4–5 minutes

Rice Stick Noodles, Rice Vermicelli: (rice flour)
always dried: soften in hot water for 15 minutes,
     then boil for 1 minute or deep-fry for
     30 seconds

Ho Fun, Rice Ribbon Noodles: (rice flour)
used in China, Malaysia, Singapore, and Thailand: similar to Vietnamese Banh Pho
fresh: soak in hot water to separate, then cook for
     1 minute
dried: cook for 2–3 minutes

Spring Roll Wrappers: (wheat flour)
also known as Lumpia Wrappers in the Philippines
always fresh: fill, then steam for 5 minutes,
     or deep-fry for 1 minute

Gyozo Wrappers: (egg, wheat flour)
always fresh: boil, steam, or fry for 5–7 minutes or
     deep-fry for 1 minute

Wonton Skins: (egg, wheat flour)
always fresh: boil for 4–5 minutes, with filling,
     or deep-fry for 1 minute

Cellophane or Beanthread Noodles:
(mung bean starch)
always dried: soften in boiling water for
     15 minutes, then boil for 1 minute or
     deep-fry for 30 seconds

Taiwanese Cellophane Noodles:
(potato starch and mung bean flour)
always dried: soften in boiling water for
     15 minutes, then boil for 1 minute or
     deep-fry for 30 seconds

Agar Agar Noodles: (seaweed)
similar to beanthread noodles
always dried: soak in boiling water until tender,
     then use with other ingredients in
     cold dishes

Shanghai Noodles: (wheat, or wheat and egg)
(1) round, fresh egg noodles, thicker than
     spaghetti—rinse in warm water, then boil
     for 1–2 minutes until tender
(2) white wheat-flour noodles, similar to
     Japanese Somen. Cook as for Somen.

korea
In Korea, as in all Asian countries, noodles symbolize longevity; Chap Chae, Kuksu, and Naengmyon are the three classic Korean noodle dishes. Naengmyon Noodles, made of buckwheat flour, are very resilient, and should be snipped with scissors into manageable lengths before eating.

Tangmyon Noodles:
(sweet potato and mung bean starch)
used in Chap Chae, the famous Korean noodle and vegetable dish: Chinese Cellophane Noodles may be substituted
always dried: soften in boiling water for
     10 minutes, then stir-fry for up to 1 minute

Naengmyon Noodles: (buckwheat flour)
used cold as a summer dish in chilled soup with beef and sliced pear
always dried: soften in boiling water for
     10 minutes, then stir-fry up to 1 minute

Son Myon Noodles: (wheat flour)
used for Kuksu (soup with noodles, meat, and vegetables): other thin wheat noodles, such as Japanese Somen may be substituted
preparation: as for Somen noodles (Japan)

japan
The cooking method for all dried Japanese noodles is the same. Bring a saucepan of water to a boil, add the noodles and return to a boil. Skim if necessary, then splash in cold water, return to a boil, then skim again. This process, which improves their texture, is repeated 2–3 times in a short cooking period. When cooked, the noodles are rinsed to remove excess starch and reheated, if necessary, by dipping in boiling water.

Soba Noodles: (buckwheat flour)
fresh: rinse in warm water, then boil for
     1–1½ minutes
dried: boil for 5–6 minutes
also available:
     Green Chasoba Noodles
     (buckwheat flour and green tea)
     Zaru Soba Noodles
     (buckwheat flour with yam starch)

Udon Noodles: (wheat flour)
fresh: rinse in warm water, then boil for
     1–2 minutes
dried: boil for 10–12 minutes

Ramen Noodles: (egg and wheat flour)
fresh: rinse in warm water, then boil for
     1–2 minutes
dried: boil for 4½–5 minutes

Somen or Hiyamugi Noodles: (wheat flour)
fresh: rinse in warm water, then boil for
     1–2 minutes
dried: boil for 2½–3 minutes
also available:
     Pink Ikeshima Shiso Somen
     (flavored with shiso leaves)
     Dark Green Ikeshima Cha Somen
     (flavored with green tea)

Harusame or "Spring Rain" Noodles:
(rice flour, though sometimes made of potato
starch or tapioca flour)
very fine noodles sold in skeins
always dried: soften in hot water for 15 minutes,
   then serve as they are or reheat

**Shirataki "White Waterfall" or "Snowed Black Bean
Curd" Noodles:** (starch of the devil's tongue plant,
related to sweet potatoes)
fine white noodles with a pleasant crunchy texture,
sold fresh in tubs of water
always fresh: rinse in warm water then add directly
   to a dish: they soften in contact
   with the sauce

thailand
Noodle dishes were introduced to
Thailand from China, and they are the only foods
eaten with chopsticks. Other foods are eaten with
the fingers, fork, and/or spoon.

There are five main varieties of Thai noodles:

Sen Yai: (rice flour)
broad flat noodles. also known as rice river
noodles or rice stick noodles.
fresh: soak in hot water to separate, then boil for
   1 minute
dried: soften in hot water for 15 minutes, then
   boil for 2–3 minutes

Ba Mee: (egg and rice flour)
sold in nests that are shaken loose before cooking
always fresh: rinse in warm water, then
   boil for 3–4 minutes

Sen Mee: (rice flour)
thin rice noodles or vermicelli
usually dried: soften in hot water for 15 minutes,
   then boil for 45 seconds

Sen Lek, Jantaboon, or Changaboon: (rice flour)
flat, medium noodles or rice sticks
usually dried; soften in hot water for 15 minutes,
   then boil for 45 seconds

Wun Sen or Cellophane Noodles: (soy bean flour)
very thin, wiry, transparent vermicelli
usually dried: soak in boiling water for 15 minutes,
   then boil for 1 minute or deep-fry 1 minute

vietnam
Most Vietnamese noodles are made
from rice flour or mung bean starch. They can be
eaten at any time of the day, alone or with other
dishes. The legendary Banh Pho used to be
confined to northern breakfasts, but is now served
throughout the day all over the country.

Banh Hoi: (rice flour)
very fine, hair-like rice sticks or vermicelli
always dried: soften in hot water for 5 minutes,
   then steam for 5 minutes

Bun: (rice flour)
thin rice vermicelli used in soups, salads, spring rolls
always dried: boil for 1–2 minutes

Banh Pho: (rice flour)
wide rice stick noodles used in Vietnamese pho
dishes such as Pho Bo and Pho Ca
fresh: rinse in warm water then add to dishes
dried: soak for 15 minutes in hot water, then boil
   for 1–2 minutes

Banh Trang: (rice flour) dried rice paper wrappers
always dried: dip in hot water for 30 seconds to
   soften, then add fillings, roll up, and serve
   as they are or deep-fry

philippines
Noodle traditions were borrowed
from the Chinese, then melded with the many
other cultural traditions of the islands, including
Spanish, Pacific Island, and local tribal dishes.

Miswa Noodles: similar to Japanese Somen or
Hiyamugi Noodles (wheat flour)
always dried: cook in simmering salted water until
   tender, then use in soups or stir-fries

Lumpia Wrappers: (see Chinese Spring Roll Wrappers)

malaysia and singapore
One of
the most famous cooking styles in Malaysia and
Singapore is Straits Chinese Nonya cooking, a
mixture of Chinese and Malay traditions.

Laksa Noodles: (rice flour)
local name for Rice Vermicelli, used fresh or dried
in spicy noodle laksas or soups, flavored with
coconut in Singapore and with lime or tamarind in
Penang. Prepare as for Chinese Rice Vermicelli.

pasta

Pasta should be cooked in a large saucepan in
at least 4 quarts of boiling salted water. Do NOT
add olive oil unless cooking ravioli or other filled
shapes which may stick together. Bring the water
to a boil, add salt, return to a boil, then add the
pasta all at once. Stir with a wooden fork or spoon,
cover, return to a boil, then remove the lid or set it
ajar to prevent boiling over. Stir from time to time
during the cooking period.

Cooking times Fresh pasta is cooked in a matter of
minutes, depending on thickness, the flour used,
the size of the saucepan, and how fast the water
is boiling.

Cooking times for dried pasta vary according to the
kind of flour used and the method of manufacture.

Use the package instructions as a guide, but start
to taste-test toward the end of the cooking time—
the texture should be *al dente*, which means "to
the tooth"—tender, but with a definite bite. There
should be no hard white core.

Drain immediately into a colander and toss with
olive oil and Parmesan, or add straight to sauce.

Stuffed or filled fresh pasta shapes are cooked
until they rise to the surface, then a little longer,
according to the size and nature of the filling.

Serving quantities As a starter, allow 2 oz. dried
pasta or 4 oz. fresh pasta per serving. As a main
course, allow 3–4 oz. dried pasta or 6–7 oz. fresh
pasta per person, depending on appetites. Less
may be required if it is being served with a very
substantial sauce.

Categories There are hundreds of pasta shapes,
many of which have been used in the recipes in
this book. Categories include:

Pasta lunga (long pasta), including spaghetti
(strings), traditionally served with olive-oil based
sauces, spaghettini (little strings), linguine (little
tongues), and bucatoni (big holes).
Fettuce (ribbons), including tagliolini (little
slices), tagliatelli (thin slices), fettucine (little
ribbons), and the wider pappardelle.
Tubi (tube-shaped) pasta include cannelloni,
rigatoni, penne, and maccheroni.
Forme speciale (special shapes) such as fusilli
(spirals), conchiglie (shells), and orecchiette (ears)
capture sauces in their twists and hollows.
Ridged shapes of any of the above varieties such
as rigatoni and penne rigate also help sauces
adhere to the surface.
Sheet pasta, of which the best known is lasagne.
Soup pasta are very small shapes such as stelline
(little stars) and orzo (little grain) which cook
quickly. They are used to thicken soups and they
look particularly attractive in clear broths.
Flavored pasta other than spinach, tomato, or nero
(black, flavored with squid ink), are not admired
by purists, though many different varieties are
available around the world, including those with
herb leaves integrated with the dough.

planning menus with noodles and pasta

soups

appetizers

cheese dishes

fish and seafood

poultry, meat, and game

vegetables

desserts

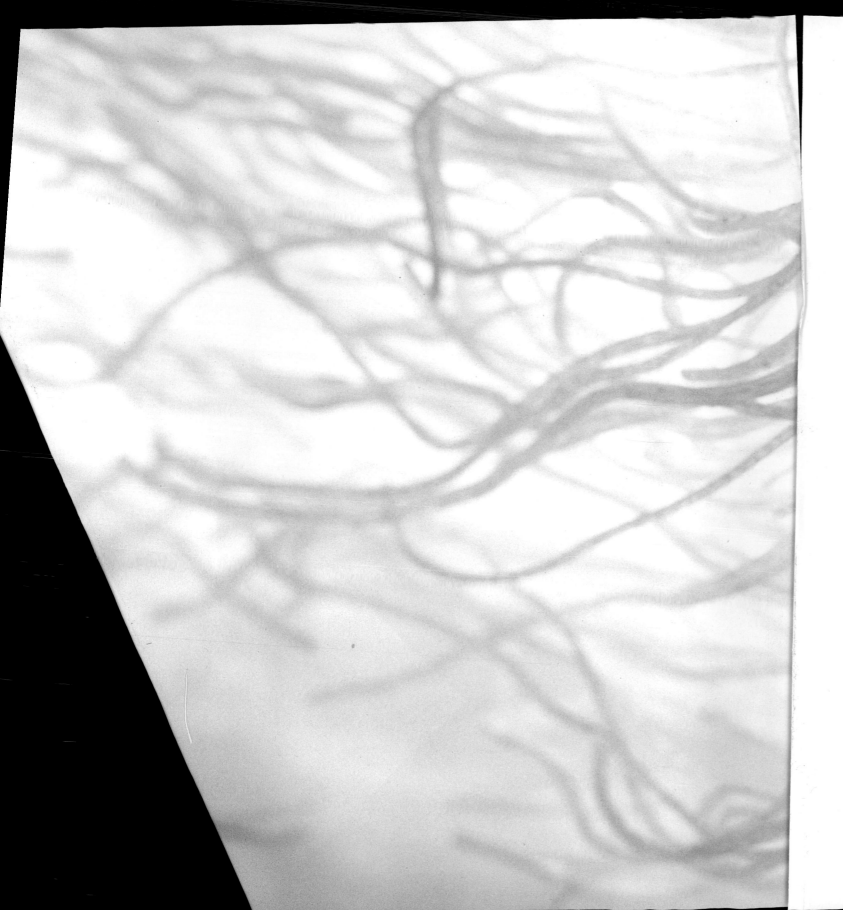

index